Praise for *Building Serverless Applications with Google Cloud Run*

"Wietse Venema's book goes into significant technical depth while also keeping the reader grounded with realistic scenarios. I had the opportunity to review it, and look forward to purchasing a copy of my own so that I can read it again. Google Cloud Run may be the most interesting compute platform you'll use in the years ahead, and this book will help you build up the knowledge you need to successfully use it."

—*Richard Seroter,*
Director of Outbound Product Management at Google Cloud

"Get ready for what I believe is going to be the de facto reference book for Google Cloud Run. Wietse Venema explores and explains every facet of the product and goes into details of building production-grade serverless apps. As a Cloud Run Product Manager, I helped review every chapter for accuracy."

—*Steren Giannini,*
Cloud Run Product Manager at Google Cloud

"This is the most comprehensive, yet approachable guide to getting started with Cloud Run (and its vast array of accompanying tools and technologies) that currently exists—no small feat for a technology that's seen rapid evolution over the past 12 months. From introducing the concept of containers, to discussing the real-world considerations when deploying Cloud Run as part of a microservices-based architecture, Wietse has written a book that will appeal to both newcomers to Google Cloud and veteran developers alike."

—*Chris Tippett,*
Principal Consultant at Servian (UK)

"What can I say. . .this guy definitely knows what he's talking about. He is as enthusiastic about the subject as most people are about little puppies, and manages to explain it in a way that anyone can understand it. His diagrams are a strong part of the book. They help you understand topics that can be daunting and difficult to comprehend, especially for junior backend developers like myself. Go buy this book, it will make your life running in the cloud a whole lot easier!"

—Femke Buijs,
Software Engineer at Mollie

"Developers looking to future proof their career for the next decade will love this book because: #1 It is a practical, easy to read and concise guide on Cloud Run (the technology that finally closes the gap between Serverless and Containers). #2 The author covers a broad set of managed services on Google Cloud Platform to help you become productive quickly (even if you're new to GCP). #3 If you're skeptical about vendor lock-in, you will appreciate the section on how to take your serverless containers and "move out" of the Google Cloud."

—Daniel Zivkovic,
Solution Architect and Organizer of Serverless Toronto User Group

"Wietse has an engaging and personal style that makes this book a pleasure to read. What I like especially, is that apart from essential knowledge about Cloud Run, it also contains plenty of anecdotes, best practices, and useful advice to make you a better application developer. Highly recommended!"

—Robbert Brak,
Principal Software Engineer at 4me

Building Serverless Applications
with Google Cloud Run

A Real-World Guide to Building
Production-Ready Services

Wietse Venema

Beijing · Boston · Farnham · Sebastopol · Tokyo 

Building Serverless Applications with Google Cloud Run

by Wietse Venema

Published by O'Reilly Media, Inc., 1005 Gravenstein Highway North, Sebastopol, CA 95472.

O'Reilly books may be purchased for educational, business, or sales promotional use. Online editions are also available for most titles (*http://oreilly.com*). For more information, contact our corporate/institutional sales department: 800-998-9938 or *corporate@oreilly.com*.

Acquisitions Editor: Jennifer Pollock	**Indexer:** Sue Klefstad
Developmental Editor: Sarah Grey	**Interior Designer:** David Futato
Production Editor: Beth Kelly	**Cover Designer:** Karen Montgomery
Copyeditor: Holly Bauer Forsyth	**Illustrator:** Wietse Venema
Proofreader: Rachel Monaghan	

December 2020: First Edition

Revision History for the First Edition

2020-12-02: First Release

See *http://oreilly.com/catalog/errata.csp?isbn=9781492057093* for release details.

978-1-492-05709-3

[LSI]

Table of Contents

Foreword. xiii

Preface. xvii

1. Introduction. 1
   Serverless Applications   1
     A Simple Developer Experience   2
     Autoscalable Out of the Box   3
     A Different Cost Model   4
     Serverless Is Not Functions as a Service   5
   Google Cloud   5
   Serverless on Google Cloud   7
   Cloud Run   8
     Service   8
     Container Image   8
     Scalability and Self-Healing   9
     HTTPS Serving   9
     Microservices Support   9
     Identity, Authentication, and Access Management   9
     Monitoring and Logging   10
     Transparent Deployments   10
     Pay-Per-Use   10
   Concerns About Serverless   10
     Unpredictable Costs   11
     Hyper-Scalability   11
     When Things Go Really Wrong   11

        Separation of Compute and Storage   11
        Open Source Compatibility   12
     Summary   12

2. Understanding Cloud Run.   13
     Getting Started with Google Cloud   13
        Costs   14
        Interacting with Google Cloud   14
        Google Cloud Projects   15
        Installing and Authenticating the SDK   15
        Installing Beta Components   16
     Deploying Your First Service   16
        Deploying the Sample Container   16
        Region   17
        Structure of the HTTPS Endpoint   18
        Viewing Your Service in the Web Console   18
        Deploying a New Version   19
        Revision   20
     Understanding Cloud Run   22
        Container Life Cycle   22
        CPU Throttling   24
        Task Scheduling and Throttling   24
        Load Balancer and Autoscaler   24
        Concurrent Request Limit   26
        Autoscaler   26
        Tuning the Concurrency Setting   27
        Cold Starts   27
        Disposable Containers   27
        In-Memory Filesystem   28
        Ready for Requests   28
        Cloud Run Key Points   28
     Choosing a Serverless Compute Product on Google Cloud   29
        Cloud Functions: Glue Code   29
        App Engine: Platform as a Service   30
        Key Differences   30
        What Will the Future Look Like?   31
     Summary   32

3. Building Containers.   33
     Containers: A Hands-On Exploration   34
        Running an Interactive Shell   34

Overriding the Default Command   35
Running a Server   35
Containers from First Principles   36
Inside a Container Image   36
The Linux Kernel   37
Container Isolation   38
Starting a Container   39
Building a Container with Docker   40
Dockerfile Instructions   41
Installing Additional Tooling   42
Smaller Is Better When Deploying to Production   43
Creating Small Containers with Distroless   43
Artifact Registry   44
Building and Tagging the Container Image   45
Authenticating and Pushing the Container Image   46
Building a Container Without a Dockerfile   46
Go Containers with ko   47
Java Containers with Jib   49
Cloud Native Buildpacks   49
Cloud Build   50
Remote Docker Build   51
Advanced Builds   51
Running Arbitrary Programs   53
Connecting with Version Control   53
Shutting Down   54
Summary   54

4. Working with a Relational Database. 55
Introducing the Demo Application   55
Creating the Cloud SQL Instance   57
Understanding Cloud SQL Proxy   58
Connecting and Loading the Schema   59
Securing the Default User   60
Connecting Cloud Run to Cloud SQL   61
Disabling the Direct Connection   62
Deploying the Demo Application   63
Connection String   64
Public and Private IP   64
Limiting Concurrency   65
Transaction Concurrency   66
Resource Contention   67

Scaling Boundaries and Connection Pooling   67
External Connection Pool   68
A Real-World Example   69
Cloud SQL in Production   69
Monitoring   69
Automatic Storage Increase   69
High Availability   69
Making Your Application Resilient Against Short Downtime   70
Shutting Down   70
Summary   70

5. **Working with HTTP Sessions**. **71**
How HTTP Sessions Work   72
Storing Sessions in Memorystore: A Hands-On Exploration   73
Creating a Memorystore Instance   73
What Is a VPC Connector?   74
Creating a VPC Connector   76
Deploying the Demo App   77
Alternative Session Stores   77
Session Affinity   78
Use Cases   79
Session Affinity Is Not for Session Data   79
Shutting Down   80
Summary   80

6. **Service Identity and Authentication**. **81**
Cloud IAM Fundamentals   81
Roles   81
Policy Binding   82
Service Accounts   85
Creating and Using a New Service Account   87
Sending Authenticated Requests to Cloud Run   88
Deploying a Private Service   88
Using an ID Token to Send Authenticated Requests   89
When Is an ID Token Valid?   90
Programmatically Calling Private Cloud Run Services   90
Google Frontend Server   91
A Story About Inter-Service Latency   92
Demo Application   92
Embedded Read-Only SQL Database   93
Running Locally   93

    Edit, Compile, Reload   94
    Deploying to Cloud Run   95
    Update the Frontend Configuration   96
    Add Custom Service Accounts   96
    Add IAM Policy Binding   96
  Summary   97

7. Task Scheduling. 99
  Cloud Tasks   99
  Hands-On Learning: A Demo Application   101
    Building the Container Images   101
    Creating a Cloud Tasks Queue   102
    Creating Service Accounts   102
    Deploying the Worker Service   102
    Deploying the Task App Service   103
    Connecting the Task Queue   103
    Scheduling a Task with the Cloud Tasks Client Library   103
    Automatic ID Token   104
    Connecting the Worker   105
    Test the App   105
  Queue Configuration   105
    Retry Configuration   105
    Rate Limiting   106
    Viewing and Updating Queue Configuration   107
  Considerations   107
    Cloud Tasks Might Deliver Your Request Twice   107
    Local Development   108
    Alternatives   108
  Summary   109

8. Infrastructure as Code Using Terraform. 111
  What Is Infrastructure as Code?   111
  Why Infrastructure as Code?   112
  Serverless Infrastructure   113
    How It Works   113
    When Not to Use Infrastructure as Code   114
  Terraform   115
    Installing Terraform   115
    Getting Started with a Minimal Example   116
  The Terraform Workflow   122
    Change with Terraform: Adding the Access Policy   124

Expressing Dependencies with References   125
Supplemental Resources   126
Summary   127

9. Structured Logging and Tracing... 129
Logging on Cloud Run   129
Viewing Logs in the Web Console   130
Viewing Logs in the Terminal   130
Finding Invisible Logs   131
Plain-Text Logs Leave You Wanting More   132
Demo Application   132
Structured Logging   132
Client Libraries   134
Structured Logging in Other Languages   134
How to Use Log Levels   134
Capturing Panics   135
Local Development   137
Request Context   137
Trace Context   139
Forwarding Trace ID   139
Preparing All Incoming Requests with the Trace ID   141
Passing Request Context to Outgoing Requests   141
Viewing Trace Context in Cloud Logging   143
Additional Resources About Tracing   143
Log-Based Metrics with Cloud Monitoring   143
Summary   144

10. Cloud Run and Knative Serving... 147
What Is Knative Serving?   148
Cloud Run Is Not Managed Knative Serving   148
Knative Serving on Google Cloud   148
Understanding Kubernetes   149
API Server   150
Kubernetes Resources   151
Database   151
Controllers   151
Adding Extensions to Kubernetes   152
Running Knative Serving Locally   152
Running a Local Kubernetes Cluster   152
Installing Minikube and kubectl   153
Starting Your Local Cluster   153

            Install the Knative Operator   154
            Starting Minikube Tunnel   155
            Installing an HTTP Load Balancer   156
            Configuring DNS   157
            Deploying a Service   157
            Deploying the Same Service to Cloud Run   158
            Alternative API Clients   158
        Shutting Down   159
        Discussion   159
            Serving   159
            Moving from Kubernetes to Cloud Run Is Harder   159
            Service Identity and Authentication   159
            Proprietary Managed Services   160
        Summary   160

Index. 161

Foreword

I started my career as the dot-com bubble was inflating. Companies set their sights on becoming "the future of [fill in the blank]" by leveraging the internet to transform how people did everything from ordering pet food to buying books. Companies rushed to build data centers, filled them with servers, and began writing the software that would go on to eat the world, but not before the bubble burst—most companies filed for bankruptcy but left the servers and a mountain of technical debt behind.

The bursting of the dot-com bubble gave birth to a universe where every company was transformed into a tech company built on top of server farms and the weeds of infrastructure that grew around them. Soon the technical debt caught up to us and forced the industry to slow down—way down—and shift focus to keeping the lights on. Instead of building innovative applications for our customers, most of us spent our time patching servers and hiding behind firewalls, while our security teams chased vulnerabilities around.

What was supposed to propel us into the future became an anchor to the past.

While our server farms were slow to evolve, the cloud came to the rescue and offered a faster, cheaper, and better alternative. Instead of racking and stacking our own servers, we could rent theirs by the hour. While this was indeed an improvement, there was still something holding us back—servers.

Automation tools came and went, each offering a better way of managing servers but still occupying too much of our time. In parallel, the application side of the industry was evolving much faster—and developers decided to take things into their own hands. They created containers, which introduced a universal way of packaging applications that no longer required servers to be configured correctly before applications could run on them.

Platforms like Docker and Kubernetes enabled the industry (particularly sysadmins) to run containerized applications across our existing servers, and eventually shed light on a set of "cloud native" patterns for doing so at scale. Kubernetes is considered a wildly successful project, but even it falls short of eliminating the challenges of running the servers underneath, which still need to be patched, configured, and maintained.

What you are holding in your hands is a peek into a serverless future, where the concept of a server has been buried under a set of cloud native abstractions and workflows dedicated to running and securing your containerized applications. This is a future where cloud providers bear the burden of managing servers, so you can focus on building innovative applications for your customers.

You may be saying to yourself, "The future is already here." You're not wrong—unfortunately, it's not evenly distributed.

In this book, Wietse Venema lays out how to adopt the future of cloud computing today. He walks you through the basics by leveraging Google's Cloud Run platform, guiding you into the shallow end of the serverless pool while teaching you how to swim through a collection of hands-on examples. Each chapter moves you closer to the deep end by building on prior lessons, helping you understand how to scale your applications without sacrificing performance, and avoiding unexpected costs as you pay as you go.

As you wade into deeper, more advanced areas, such as the challenges of sharing a pool with others, Wietse keeps a steady watch as your lifeguard. Wietse highlights critical security concerns and how to address them using network policies and fine-grained IAM permissions. His pragmatic approach keeps you from drowning in complexity.

As with most serverless platforms, Cloud Run represents what most would consider a *black box*: the cloud provider owns and runs the infrastructure responsible for running your applications, and you'll need to trust them to do their part. Wietse doesn't leave you to make a leap of faith. Instead he teaches you how to "trust but verify" by leveraging the cornerstones of observability: structured logging, metrics, and tracing.

The other drawback of most serverless platforms is *vendor lock-in*. Depending on the platform, your applications may only run within a specific cloud provider's offering. While some consider worries of lock-in to be fearmongering, it's a valid concern for any practitioner. Wietse outlines how to craft applications that run well not only on Google's fully managed Cloud Run offering but on its open source counterpart, Knative, which leverages the same underlying contract for running serverless applications on top of Kubernetes, the industry standard container orchestration platform.

I've been fortunate enough to be a part of the Google team that helped create Knative and bring Cloud Run to market. I've watched Cloud Run mature as a product over the years. I've onboarded thousands of customers and I wrote a framework to help Go developers build Cloud Run applications faster—and even I learned a thing or two from this book. What took me three years to learn, Wietse delivers in less than a dozen chapters.

— Kelsey Hightower
Principal Engineer, Google Cloud

Preface

When I learned about Cloud Run in April 2019, I quickly recognized that this was a product that would radically simplify building, deploying, and scaling 'cloud native' web applications.

Public cloud has provided the opportunity to developers and businesses to turn physical servers and data centers into virtual ones. However, virtual machines and virtual networks are still a relatively low-level abstraction. You can take an even bigger leap if you design your application to take full advantage of the modern cloud platform. Cloud Run provides a higher level of abstraction over the actual server infrastructure and lets you focus on code, not infrastructure.

This book is the practical guide you can use to get started with Cloud Run.

Why I Wrote This Book

In my day job as a consultant for Binx.io I work as an engineer and trainer. A large part of my job is about developing a deep understanding about how technology works and teaching what I learned to others, so they can build better systems.

For me, publishing this book is a way to reach more people and help them get ahead. I wrote this book for you! This book will help advance your understanding, so you can become more effective in your day job. I'm hoping that will lead you to more enjoyment and new opportunities. If you're inspired by my book, I would love to connect and learn more about you! Send me a message on Twitter (*https://twitter.com/wietsevenema*), my DMs are open.

Who This Book Is For

If you build, maintain or deploy web applications, this book is for you. You might go by the title of a software engineer, a developer, system administrator, solution architect, or a cloud engineer. I carefully balance hands-on demonstrations with deep dives into the fundamentals so that you'll get value out of my book whether you're an aspiring, junior, or experienced developer.

Why Use the Go Language?

The few code listings in this book use Go, a programming language designed by Google. It is well suited to developing serverless software and its syntax is easy to understand, which makes it a good language to use for code listings.

With Go, you can produce performant, self-contained programs that use few resources. Critically, Go also makes it easy to build programs that start very fast. This is a benefit when building containers that start on-demand to handle incoming requests.

Navigating This Book

This book is organized as follows. Chapter 1, *Introduction*, gives a general overview of what a serverless application is, introduces you to Google Cloud and their serverless products without going too much in depth. If you are new to Google Cloud, this will be a great introduction.

Chapter 2, *Understanding Cloud Run*, is a hands-on introduction to Cloud Run. I'll show you how to get started with Google Cloud and deploy your first Cloud Run service. After that you upgrade your service to a next version and change configuration. While the first part of the chapter focuses on using Cloud Run, in the second part I explain the runtime characteristics of Cloud Run and how they influence the way you build your application. I'll also compare Cloud Run with the other serverless runtimes on Google Cloud: App Engine and Cloud Functions.

In Chapter 3, *Building Containers*, you'll find a thorough introduction to application development with containers. In this chapter I show you how to run containers on your local machine with Docker, create your own container images (with and without Docker), and dive into the fundamentals of containers.

The containers on Cloud Run are disposable. This requires you to store data you need to persist beyond the lifetime of a single request in a database or another downstream system. In Chapter 4, *Working with a Relational Database*, I dive into the managed product Cloud SQL (managed relational databases such as MySQL and PostgreSQL), in Chapter 5, *Working with HTTP Sessions*, I follow up with MemoryStore (Redis). I discuss scalability and reliability, as Cloud Run can scale to 1,000 containers very fast. You can even call it hyper-scalable.

Especially if you are building a more serious application, you'll want to make sure that every Cloud Run service in your system only has the permissions to do exactly what it needs to do. In information security, this is also known as the principle of least privilege: it helps to reduce the impact of a vulnerability in one part of the system.

This is why I introduce you to Cloud Identity and Access Management (IAM) in Chapter 6, *Service Identity and Authentication*. This chapter features a practical demo of two Cloud Run services, where only one service receives public traffic, and the other is protected using Cloud IAM.

Most applications have the need to schedule tasks to be executed later, either immediately after handling an HTTP request or at a scheduled time. In Chapter 7, *Task Scheduling*, I introduce you to Cloud Tasks when I cover patterns to use for task scheduling.

In Chapter 8, *Infrastructure as Code Using Terraform*, I'll show you how to work with Terraform, an infrastructure as code (IaC) tool. Terraform lets you recreate your entire project using one command, which proves useful if your application grows beyond "Hello World". If you are still getting started with building applications, you might want to skip this chapter and the last two chapters for now, to come back to them later.

I want to make sure that you have proper visibility over what is going on in your system when you go live for end users. This is why I cover structured logging and tracing in Chapter 9, *Structured Logging and Tracing*. Doing this right is fundamentally important when you run a system in production.

Finally, I move beyond the day-to-day concerns and think about the future in Chapter 10, *Cloud Run and Knative Serving*. If you build your application on top of a vendor-controlled platform, you should consider portability.

Conventions Used in This Book

The following typographical conventions are used in this book:

Italic

Indicates new terms, URLs, email addresses, filenames, and file extensions.

`Constant width`

Used for program listings, as well as within paragraphs to refer to program elements such as variable or function names, databases, data types, environment variables, statements, and keywords.

`Constant width bold`

Shows commands or other text that should be typed literally by the user.

`Constant width italic`

Shows text that should be replaced with user-supplied values or by values determined by context.

This element signifies a tip or suggestion.

This element signifies a general note.

This element indicates a warning or caution.

Using Code Examples

Supplemental material (code examples, exercises, etc.) is available for download at *https://wietsevenema.eu/cloud-run-book*.

If you have a technical question or a problem using the code examples, please send email to *bookquestions@oreilly.com*.

This book is here to help you get your job done. In general, if example code is offered with this book, you may use it in your programs and documentation. You do not need to contact us for permission unless you're reproducing a significant portion of the code. For example, writing a program that uses several chunks of code from this book does not require permission. Selling or distributing examples from O'Reilly books does require permission. Answering a question by citing this book and quoting example code does not require permission. Incorporating a significant amount of example code from this book into your product's documentation does require permission.

We appreciate, but generally do not require, attribution. An attribution usually includes the title, author, publisher, and ISBN. For example: "*Building Serverless Applications with Google Cloud Run* by Wietse Venema (O'Reilly). Copyright 2021 Wietse Venema, 978-1-492-05709-3."

If you feel your use of code examples falls outside fair use or the permission given above, feel free to contact us at *permissions@oreilly.com*.

O'Reilly Online Learning

 For more than 40 years, *O'Reilly Media* has provided technology and business training, knowledge, and insight to help companies succeed.

Our unique network of experts and innovators share their knowledge and expertise through books, articles, and our online learning platform. O'Reilly's online learning platform gives you on-demand access to live training courses, in-depth learning paths, interactive coding environments, and a vast collection of text and video from O'Reilly and 200+ other publishers. For more information, visit *http://oreilly.com*.

How to Contact Us

Please address comments and questions concerning this book to the publisher:

O'Reilly Media, Inc.
1005 Gravenstein Highway North
Sebastopol, CA 95472
800-998-9938 (in the United States or Canada)
707-829-0515 (international or local)
707-829-0104 (fax)

We have a web page for this book, where we list errata, examples, and any additional information. You can access this page at *https://oreil.ly/BSA*.

Email *bookquestions@oreilly.com* to comment or ask technical questions about this book.

For news and information about our books and courses, visit *http://oreilly.com*.

Find us on Facebook: *http://facebook.com/oreilly*

Follow us on Twitter: *http://twitter.com/oreillymedia*

Watch us on YouTube: *http://youtube.com/oreillymedia*

Acknowledgments

Writing a book (especially your first one) is a daunting project, and even more so in the year 2020. No author writes a book alone. My name is on the cover of this book, but behind me is a team of invisible supporters—and they were just as crucial to completing this work as I was.

Imagine receiving an email or a direct message on Twitter from someone you don't know and have never heard of, who is writing a book and wants your help. What would you do? I learned that a lot of people will say "Sure, how can I help?" out of generosity and kindness. I feel grateful for meeting all those wonderful people along the way. Some of you spent hours with my drafts or diagrams and helped me improve, reflect, and learn new things. Most of you I've never even met in person. I hope we do meet at some point!

A lot of people helped me with chapter reviews, commented on my diagrams, encouraged me, or helped me find the right people to connect with. Because of them, this book is of considerable better quality. In alphabetical order, thank you to:

Albert Brand, Armon Dadgar, Arne Timmerman, Bart Kooijman, Benjamin Komen, Bill Kennedy, Carl Tanner, Daniel Zivkovic, David Linthicum, Dean Shanahan, Femke Buijs, Graham Polley, Greg Wilson, Jason Polites, Jeff Bleiel, Joe Beda, Karolína Netolická, Kerim Satirli, Kyle Ruddy, Lak Lakshmanan, Liz Rice, Nagalenoj Hari-NagaSampath, Mattijs Bliek, Mike Truty, Oren Teich, Taylor Dolezal, Thijs Elferink, Tein de Vries, Vinod Ramachandran.

I also want to thank the management teams at Binx and Xebia for their support. Thank you for helping me find time to write in spite of work commitments, and creating a great company culture that supported me in conceiving and executing this moonshot plan to write an O'Reilly book: Andrew de la Haije, Bart Verlaat, Daan Teunissen, Elaine Versloot, Martijn Botermans, Mark van Holstein, Walter van der Scheer.

To the production team at O'Reilly, thank you for turning my drafts into a tangible book, and for making the process smooth: Beth Kelly, Holly Bauer Forsyth, Rachel Monaghan, Sue Klefstad, Rob Romano, and David Futato.

Christopher Chedeau and David Lužar, thank you for starting the open source project excalidraw (the tool I used to create the drawings in this book). Your tool was invaluable to my thinking process.

I want to extend a special thanks to Abdellfetah Sghiouar, Cen Liu, Jose Andrade, and Suchit Puri from Google PSO. You've helped me from the beginning, and you were instrumental in helping me grow to become an O'Reilly author. Abdel, you went to great depth to review all chapters, even when I was sending you one chapter every week when the deadline was near. Thank you!

Robbert Brak, thank you for being such a great friend and mentor, especially when I just started writing this book. Your feedback was always very thoughtful and honest. You are the only one who read all the chapters, and then the chapters that didn't make it into the book, and all chapter revisions. It's a fact that this book would not have existed without your support.

Richard Seroter, thank you so much for reviewing the entire book. Your support, encouragement, and critical thinking really helped me get to the finish line.

Chris Tippett, you're just the friendliest random stranger I've ever met on the internet. Thank you so much for supporting me in the last mile! Here's a promise to you: if you write your book, I'll review every single page!

Kathleen Carr, thank you for recognizing something in me that I didn't even see at that point. Your support, kindness and trust from the start meant a lot to me.

Jennifer Pollock, thank you for bringing the book home in the middle of a pandemic.

Steren Giannini, thank you for tirelessly answering all my questions, reviewing my diagrams and helping me make sure everything I wrote was correct.

Yuki Furuyama, I reached out to you with a few simple questions at a moment's notice, just before my final deadline. You did not only answer my questions, but went to considerable depth to resolve a fundamental issue you saw with the chapter. Thank you so much for your kindness and valuable insights. Chapter 9 wouldn't have been what it is today without you.

Kelsey Hightower, I feel grateful for your support and encouragement and I want to thank you for writing an amazing foreword. Your leadership has been an inspiration to me, and to many others in the tech community.

Sarah Grey, you know I wouldn't have finished the book without you. I learned so much from you and I have to say one thing: I still don't know how you managed to make me stick to the schedule. I really miss our editorial review sessions—they were very gezellig as well as productive.

Davy Landman, you taught me how to create proper diagrams. If there is an unlabeled arrow in this book it is solely my fault. I also clearly remember a pivotal meeting in December 2019 when you helped me structure the tangled mess that was my manuscript at that point. And most importantly, thank you for being my best friend.

Thank you, Annemieke, Merel, and Jasmijn, for understanding and putting up with all the hours (and nights) I spent writing and coding. You are the reason why it's all worth it.

## CHAPTER 1

Introduction

Cloud Run is a platform on Google Cloud that lets you build scalable and reliable web-based applications. As a developer, you can get very close to being able to just write your code and push it, and then let the platform deploy, run, and scale your application for you.

Public cloud has provided the opportunity to developers and businesses to turn physical servers and data centers into virtual ones, greatly decreasing lead time and turning big, up-front investments in physical servers and data centers into ongoing operational expenses. For most businesses, this is already a great step forward.

However, virtual machines and virtual networks are still a relatively low-level abstraction. You can take an even bigger leap if you design your application to take full advantage of the modern cloud platform. Cloud Run provides a higher level of abstraction over the actual server infrastructure and allows you to focus on code, not infrastructure.

Using the higher-level abstraction that Cloud Run provides doesn't mean you tie yourself to Google Cloud forever. First, Cloud Run requires your application to be packaged in a container—a portable way to deploy and run your application. If your container runs on Cloud Run, you can also run it on your own server, using Docker, for instance. Second, the Cloud Run platform is based on the open Knative specification, which means you can migrate your applications to another vendor or your own hardware with limited effort.

Serverless Applications

You probably bought this book because you are interested in building a serverless application. It makes sense to be specific about what *application* means, because it is a very broad term; your phone runs applications, and so does a server. This book is about web-based applications, which receive requests (or events) over HTTPS and respond to them.

Examples of web-based applications include the sites you interact with using a web browser and APIs you can program against. These are the two primary use cases I focus on in this book. You can also build event processing pipelines and workflow automation with Cloud Run.

One thing I want to emphasize is that when I say HTTP, I refer to the entire family of HTTP protocols, including HTTP/2 (the more advanced and performant version). If you are interested in reading more about the evolution of HTTP, I suggest you read this well-written overview at MDN (*https://oreil.ly/_jm93*).

Now that I have scoped down what "application" means in the context of this book, let's take a look at serverless. If you use serverless components to build your application, your application is serverless. But what does *serverless* mean? It's an abstract and overloaded term that means different things to different people.

When trying to understand serverless, you shouldn't focus too much on the "no servers" part—it's more than that. In general, this is what I think people mean when they call something serverless and why they are excited about it:

- It simplifies the developer experience by eliminating the need to manage infrastructure.
- It's scalable out of the box.
- Its cost model is "pay-per-use": you pay exactly for what you use, not for capacity you reserve up front. If you use nothing, you pay nothing.

In the next sections, I'll explore these three aspects of serverless in more depth.

A Simple Developer Experience

Eliminating infrastructure management means you can focus on writing your code and have someone else worry about deploying, running, and scaling your application. The platform will take care of all the important and seemingly simple details that are surprisingly hard to get right, like autoscaling, fault tolerance, logging, monitoring, upgrades, deployment, and failover.

One thing you specifically *don't* have to do in the serverless context is infrastructure management. The platform offers an abstraction layer. This is the primary reason we call it serverless.

When you are running a small system, infrastructure management might not seem like a big deal, but readers who manage more than 10 servers know that this can be a significant responsibility that takes a lot of work to get right. Here is an incomplete list of tasks you no longer need to perform when you run your application logic on a serverless platform:

- Provisioning and configuring servers (or setting up automation)
- Applying security patches to your servers
- Configuring networking and firewalls
- Setting up SSL/TLS certificates, updating them yearly, and configuring a web server
- Automating application deployment on a cluster of servers
- Building automation that can handle hardware failures transparently
- Setting up logging and metrics monitoring to provide insights into system performance

And that's just about servers! Most businesses have higher and higher expectations for system availability. More than 30 minutes of downtime per month is generally unacceptable. To reach these levels of availability, you will need to automate your way out of every failure mode—there is not enough time for manual troubleshooting. As you can imagine, this is a lot of work and leads to more complexity in your infrastructure. If you build software in an enterprise environment, you'll have an easier time getting approvals from security and operations teams because a lot of their responsibilities shift to the vendor.

Availability is also related to software deployments now that it is more common to deploy new software versions on a daily basis instead of monthly. When you deploy your application, you don't want to experience downtime, even when the deployment fails.

Serverless technology helps you focus on solving your business problems and building a great product while someone else worries about the fundamentals of running your app. This sounds very convenient, but you shouldn't take this to mean that all your responsibilities disappear. Most importantly, you still need to write and patch your code and make sure it is secure and correct. There is still some configuration you need to manage, too, like setting resource requirements, adding scaling boundaries, and configuring access policies.

Autoscalable Out of the Box

Serverless products are built to increase and decrease their capacity automatically, closely tracking demand. The scale of the cloud ensures that your application will be able to handle almost any load you throw at it. A key feature of serverless is that it shows stable and consistent performance, regardless of scale.

One of our clients runs a fairly popular soccer site in the Netherlands. The site has a section that shows live scores, which means they experience peak loads during matches. When a popular match comes up, they provision more servers and add them to the instance pool. Then, when the match is over, they remove the virtual machines again to save costs. This has generally worked well for them, and they saw little reason to change things.

However, they were not prepared when one of our national clubs suddenly did very well in the UEFA Champions League. Contrary to all expectations, this club reached the semifinals. While all soccer fans in the Netherlands were uniting in support of the team, our client experienced several outages, which couldn't be solved by adding more servers.

The point is that, while you might not feel the drawbacks of a serverful system right now, you might need the scalability benefits of serverless in the future when you need to handle unforeseen circumstances. Most systems have the tendency to scale just fine until they hit a bottleneck and performance suddenly degrades. The architecture of Cloud Run provides you with guardrails that help you avoid common mistakes and build more scalable applications by default.

A Different Cost Model

The cost model of serverless is different: you pay for actual usage only, not for the preallocation of capacity. When you are not handling requests on a serverless platform, you pay nothing. On Cloud Run, you pay for the system resources you use to handle a request with a granularity of 100 ms and a small fee for every million requests. Pay-per-use can also apply to other types of products. With a serverless database, you pay for every query and for the data you store.

I present this with a caveat: I am *not* claiming that serverless is cheap. While most early adopters seem to experience a cost reduction, in some cases, serverless might turn out to be more expensive. One of these cases is when you currently manage to utilize close to 100% of your server capacity all of the time. I think this is very rare; utilization rates of 20 to 40% are much more common. That's a lot of idle servers that you are paying for.

The serverless cost model provides the vendor with an incentive to make sure your application scales fast and is always available. They have skin in the game.

This is how that works: you pay for the resources you actually use, which means your vendor wants to make sure your application handles every request that comes in. As soon as your vendor drops a request, they potentially fail to monetize their server resources.

Serverless Is Not Functions as a Service

People often associate serverless with functions as a service (FaaS) products such as Cloud Functions or AWS Lambda. With FaaS, you typically use a function as "glue code" to connect and extend existing Google Cloud services. Functions use a runtime framework: you deploy a small snippet of code, not a container. In the snippet of code, you implement only one function or override a method, which handles an incoming request or an event. You're not starting an HTTP server yourself.

FaaS is serverless because it has a simple developer experience—you don't need to worry about the runtime of your code (other than configuring the programming language) or about creating and managing the HTTPS endpoint. Scaling is built in, and you pay a small fee per one million requests.

As you will discover in this book, Cloud Run is serverless, but it has more capabilities than a FaaS platform. Serverless is also not limited to handling HTTPS requests. The other primitives you use to build your application can be serverless as well. Before I give an overview of the other serverless products on Google Cloud, it's now time to introduce Google Cloud itself.

Google Cloud

Google Cloud started in 2008 when Google released App Engine, a serverless application platform. App Engine was serverless before we started using the word *serverless*. However, back then, the App Engine runtime had a lot of limitations, which in practice meant that it was only suitable for new projects. Some people loved it, some didn't. Notable customer success stories include Snapchat and Spotify. App Engine got limited traction in the market.

Prompted by this lukewarm reaction to App Engine and a huge market demand for virtual server infrastructure, Google Cloud released Compute Engine in 2012. (That's a solid six years *after* Amazon launched EC2, the product that runs virtual machines on AWS.) This leads me to believe that the Google mindset has always been serverless.

Here's another perspective: a few years ago, Google published a paper about Borg, the global container infrastructure on which they run most of their software, including Google Search, Gmail, and Compute Engine (that's how you run virtual machines).[1] Here's how they describe it (emphasis mine):

---

1 Verma Abhishek et al., "Large-scale cluster management at Google with Borg" (*https://oreil.ly/V0qkB*), *Proceedings of EuroSys* (2015).

Borg provides three main benefits: it (1) hides the details of resource management and failure handling so its users can *focus on application development instead*; (2) operates with very high reliability and availability, and supports applications that do the same; and (3) lets us run workloads across tens of thousands of machines effectively.

Let this sink in for a bit: Google has been working on planet-scale container infrastructure since at least 2005, based on the few public accounts on Borg. A primary design goal of the Borg system is to allow developers to focus on application development instead of the operational details of running software and to scale to tens of thousands of machines. That's not just scalable, it's hyper-scalable.

If you were developing and running software at the scale that Google does, would you want to be bothered with maintaining a serverful infrastructure, let alone worry about basic building blocks like IP addresses, networks, and servers?

By now it should be clear that I like to work with Google Cloud. That's why I'm writing a book about building serverless applications with Google Cloud Run. I will not be comparing it with other cloud vendors, such as Amazon and Microsoft, because I lack the deep expertise in other cloud platforms that would be required to make such a comparison worth reading. However, rest assured, the general application design principles you will pick up in this book do translate well to other platforms.

Sustainability

It's worth noting that Google has a particular advantage when it comes to environmental sustainability. I'm writing this book in 2020, a year with a global pandemic, record-breaking heat waves all over the world, and a wildfire season that never seems to stop. Hurricanes, lightning storms, floods, and snowstorms are getting more extreme and are undeniably linked to human activity and the way we produce and consume energy. Datacenter infrastructure consumes a lot of energy to run servers— and to keep them cool.

Google Cloud has been carbon neutral since 2007 and matched its energy use with 100% renewable energy in 2017. Their aim is to be completely carbon free in 2030 (*https://oreil.ly/D1Aqg*).

Carbon neutrality is achieved by buying carbon offsets. Critics say that it's not clear that carbon offsets actually reduce carbon emissions. *Renewable energy match* means you still use energy from fossil fuels but match that with clean energy purchases (this actually reduces carbon emissions). *Carbon free* is when you use only carbon-free energy at any point in time.

According to a 2019 Wired report (*https://oreil.ly/3kKQn*), neither Microsoft Azure nor Amazon is close to achieving 100% renewable energy match, and Amazon is being criticized for not even providing a clear timeline toward that goal.

Serverless on Google Cloud

Take a look at Table 1-1 for an overview of Google Cloud serverless products that relate to application development. I've also noted information on each one's open source compatibility to indicate if there are open source alternatives you can host on a different provider. This is important, because vendor tie-in is the number-one concern with serverless. Cloud Run does well on this aspect because it is API compatible with an open source product.

Table 1-1. Serverless products on Google Cloud related to application development

Product	Purpose	Open source compatibility
Messaging		
Pub/Sub	Events	Proprietary[1]
Cloud Tasks	Delayed tasks	Proprietary[1]
Cloud Scheduler	Scheduled tasks	Proprietary[1]
Events for Cloud Run	Events	OSS compatible
Compute		
Cloud Run	Container platform	OSS compatible
App Engine	Application platform	Proprietary[2]
Cloud Functions	Connecting existing Google Cloud services	Proprietary[2]
Data Storage		
Cloud Storage	Blob storage	Proprietary[3]
Firestore	Key-value store	Proprietary

1. If you are careful, you can maintain a feasible upgrade path to OSS alternatives.
2. For most programming languages, an easy upgrade path exists to Cloud Run and other Knative-based environments because of the open source runtimes.
3. There are OSS and proprietary alternatives that implement similar APIs for blob storage.

Notably missing from the serverless offering on Google Cloud is a relational database. I think there are a lot of applications out there for which using a relational database makes a lot of sense, and most readers are already familiar with this form of application architecture. This is why I'll show you how to use Cloud SQL, a managed relational database, in Chapter 4. As a managed service, it provides many of the benefits of serverless but does not scale automatically. In addition, you pay for the capacity you allocate, even if you do not use it.

Cloud Run

Cloud Run is a serverless platform that runs and scales your container-based application. It is implemented directly on top of Borg, the hyper-scalable container infrastructure that Google uses to power Google Search, Maps, Gmail, and App Engine.

The developer workflow is a straightforward three-step process. First, you write your application using your favorite programming language. Your app should start an HTTP server. Second, you build and package your application into a container image. The third and final step is to deploy the container image to Cloud Run. Cloud Run creates a *service* resource and returns an invokable HTTPS endpoint to you (Figure 1-1).

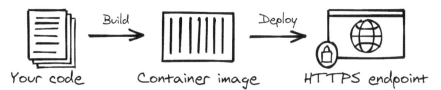

Figure 1-1. Cloud Run developer workflow

Service

I want to pause here and direct your attention to the word *service*, because this is a key concept in Cloud Run. Every service has a unique name and an associated HTTPS endpoint. You'll interact primarily with a service resource to perform your tasks, such as deploying a new container image, rolling back to a previously deployed version, and changing configuration settings like environment variables and scaling boundaries.

Container Image

Depending on how far you are in your learning journey, you might not know what a container image is. If you do know what it is, you might associate container technology with a lot of low-level infrastructure overhead that you are not remotely interested in learning. I want to reassure you: you don't need to become a container expert in order to be productive with Cloud Run. Depending on your use case, you might never have to build a container image yourself. However, understanding what containers are and how they work is certainly helpful. I'll cover containers from first principles in Chapter 3.

For now, it's enough to understand that a container image is a package that contains your application and everything it needs to run. The mental model that "a container image contains a program you can start" works well for understanding this chapter.

Cloud Run is not just a convenient way to launch a container. The platform has additional features that make it a suitable platform for running a major production system. The rest of this section will give you an overview of those features and help you understand some of Cloud Run's most important aspects. Then, in Chapter 2, I'll explore Cloud Run in depth.

Scalability and Self-Healing

Incoming requests to your Cloud Run service will be served by your container. If necessary, Cloud Run will add additional instances of your container to handle all incoming requests. If a single container fails, Cloud Run will replace it with a new instance. By default, Cloud Run can add up to a thousand container instances per service, and you can further raise this limit via a quota increase. The scale of the cloud really works with you here. If you need to scale out to tens of thousands of containers, that might be possible—the architecture of Cloud Run is designed to be limited only by the available capacity in a given Google Cloud region (a physical datacenter).

HTTPS Serving

By default, Cloud Run automatically creates a unique HTTPS endpoint you can use to reach your container. You can also use your own domain or hook your service into the virtual networking stack of Google Cloud if you need more advanced integrations with existing applications running on-premises or on virtual machines on Google Cloud, or with features like DDoS mitigation and a Web Application Firewall.

You can also create internal Cloud Run services that are not publicly accessible. These are great to receive events on from other Google Cloud products, for example, when a file is uploaded to a Cloud Storage bucket.

Microservices Support

Cloud Run supports the microservices model where you break your application into smaller services that communicate using API calls or event queues. This can help you scale your engineering organization, and can possibly lead to improved scalability. I cover an example of multiple services working together in Chapter 6.

Identity, Authentication, and Access Management

Every Cloud Run service has an assigned identity, which you can use to call Cloud APIs and other Cloud Run services from within the container. You can set up access policies that govern which identities can invoke your service.

Especially if you are building a more serious application, an identity system is important. You'll want to make sure that every Cloud Run service only has the permissions to do what it is supposed to do (principle of least privilege) and that the service can only be invoked by the identities that are supposed to invoke it.

For example, if your payment service gets a request to confirm a payment, you want to know who sent that request, and you want to be sure that only the payment service can access the database that stores payment data. In Chapter 6, I explore service identity and authentication in more depth.

Monitoring and Logging

Cloud Run captures standard container and request metrics, like request duration and CPU usage, and your application logs are forwarded to Cloud Logging. If you use structured logs, you can add metadata that will help you debug issues in production. In Chapter 9, I will get to the bottom of structured logs with a practical example.

Transparent Deployments

I don't know about you, but personally, having to endure slow or complicated deployments raises my anxiety. I'd say watching a thriller movie is comparable. You can double that if I need to perform a lot of orchestration on my local machine to get it right. On Cloud Run, deployments and configuration changes don't require a lot of hand-holding, and more advanced deployment strategies such as a gradual rollout or blue-green deployments are supported out of the box. If you make sure your app is ready for new requests within seconds after starting the container, you will reduce the time it takes to deploy a new version.

Pay-Per-Use

Cloud Run charges you for the resources (CPU and memory) your containers use when they serve requests. Even if Cloud Run, for some reason, decides to keep your container running when it is not serving requests, you will not pay for it. Surprisingly enough, Cloud Run keeps those idling containers running much longer than you would expect. I'll explain this in more detail in Chapter 2.

Concerns About Serverless

So far, I've only highlighted the reasons why you would want to adopt serverless. But you should be aware that, while serverless solves certain problems, it also creates new ones. Let's talk about what you should be concerned about. What risks do you take when adopting serverless, and what can you do about them?

Unpredictable Costs

The cost model is different with serverless, and this means the architecture of your system has a more direct and visible influence on the running costs of your system. Additionally, with rapid autoscaling comes the risk of unpredictable billing. If you run a serverless system that scales elastically, then when big demand comes, it will be served, and you will pay for it. Just like performance, security, and scalability, costs are now a quality aspect of your code that you need to be aware of and that you as a developer can control.

Don't let this paragraph scare you: you can set boundaries to scaling behavior and fine-tune the amount of resources that are available to your containers. You can also perform load testing to predict cost.

Hyper-Scalability

Cloud Run can scale out to a lot of container instances very quickly. This can cause trouble for downstream systems that cannot increase capacity as quickly or that have trouble serving a highly concurrent workload, such as traditional relational databases and external APIs with enforced rate limits. In Chapter 4, I will investigate how you can protect your relational database from too much concurrency.

When Things Go Really Wrong

When you run your software on top of a platform you do not own and control, you are at the mercy of your provider when things go really wrong. I don't mean when your code has an everyday bug that you can easily spot and fix. By "really wrong," I mean when, for example, your software breaks in production and you have no way to reproduce the fault when you run it locally because the bug is really in the vendor-controlled platform.

On a traditional server-based infrastructure, when you are confronted with an error or performance issue you can't explain, you can take a look under the hood because you control the entire stack. There is an abundance of tools that can help you figure out what is happening, even in production. On a vendor-controlled platform, all you can do is file a support ticket.

Separation of Compute and Storage

If you use Cloud Run, you need to store data that needs to be persisted externally in a database or on blob storage. This is called *separation of compute and storage*, and it is how Cloud Run realizes scalability. However, for workloads that benefit from fast, random access to a lot of data (that can't fit in RAM), this can add latency to request processing. This is mitigated in part by the internal networking inside of a Google Cloud datacenter, which is generally very fast with low latency.

Open Source Compatibility

Portability is important—you want to be able to migrate your application from one vendor to another, without being confronted with great challenges. While I was writing this chapter, the CIOs of a hundred large companies in the Netherlands raised the alarm (*https://oreil.ly/yMBt9*) about their software suppliers changing terms and conditions unilaterally, then imposing audits and considerable extra charges on the companies. I think this illustrates perfectly why it is important to "have a way out" and make sure a supplier never gets that kind of leverage. Even though you trust Google today, you never know what the future holds.

There are two reasons why Cloud Run is portable. First, it's container based. If a container runs on Cloud Run, it can run on any container engine, anywhere. Second, if you've built a complex distributed application with a lot of Cloud Run services that work together, you might be concerned about the portability of the platform itself. Cloud Run is API compatible with the Knative open source product. This means that you can migrate from Cloud Run to a self-hosted Kubernetes cluster (the open source container platform) with Knative installed with limited effort.[2] Kubernetes is the de facto standard when you want to deploy containers on a cluster of servers.

In your own datacenter, you are in full control of your infrastructure, but your developers still have a "serverless" developer experience if you run Knative. In Chapter 10, I explore Knative in more detail.

Summary

In this first chapter, you learned what serverless actually means and what its key characteristics are. You also got an overview of Google Cloud and saw that serverless is not limited to applications that handle HTTPS requests. Databases and task queues can be serverless, too.

Serverless is great for you if you value a simple and fast developer experience, and when you don't want to build and maintain traditional server infrastructure. The servers are still there—you just don't have to manage them anymore.

Your application will still be portable if you choose Cloud Run. It is container based, and the Cloud Run platform itself is based on the open Knative specification.

You might still have a lot of questions after reading this first chapter. That's a good thing! As you join me on this serverless journey, I encourage you to forget everything you've ever learned about managing server infrastructure.

---

2 Be careful not to tie in your application source code to Google Cloud services too closely without OSS alternatives, or you could lose the portability benefit.

## CHAPTER 2

Understanding Cloud Run

Now that you've read Chapter 1, you're ready to deploy your first container on Cloud Run. This chapter offers a practical exploration of Cloud Run. I'll start with the prerequisites and the tooling you need to install on your local machine. You'll deploy a sample container, upgrade it to a new version, and change its configuration. I'll also illustrate some of the more advanced features.

Once you've had your first experience working with Cloud Run, it will be time for a more fundamental discussion of the platform and its runtime characteristics. Running a container on Cloud Run is not the same as running that container on a traditional, always-on server. Cloud Run is request driven, uses disposable containers, and supports fast autoscaling. I will tell you what that means, how that helps you build reliable and scalable applications, and what the consequences are for your application design.

I'll close the chapter with a discussion of alternative ways to run application logic on Google Cloud using a serverless model and share my speculations about the future of Cloud Run with you.

Getting Started with Google Cloud

To work along with the examples in this book, you need to create a Google Cloud account, create a project, and install the Google Cloud CLI on your local machine.

You can sign up here (*https://oreil.ly/CiRcS*) for a Google Cloud account. There is a free trial with credits waiting for you, but you need to set up payment details. Google Cloud uses your information to prevent misuse. You can prevent actual charges to your account if you activate the free credits.

Costs

Make sure you enable the free credits because they come with a safety net to prevent unwanted charges. When you've spent the $300 in free credits, your account will be suspended and you'll need to actively reactivate your account to continue. Be aware that you will be charged after that point, and you can configure budgets and alerts.

All serverless products on Google Cloud have a generous always-free tier. On Cloud Run, the free tier means that if you use it for development, you will stay within the limits.

Not all products I review in this book have a free tier. Cloud SQL and Memorystore don't, and you can use the free credits for these. I will take care to warn you when you are creating resources that do not have a free tier. Every chapter where it's applicable has a section called "Shutting Down" that tells you what to do to prevent charges.

 Be sure to read the content at cloud.google.com/free for up-to-date information.

Interacting with Google Cloud

Once you've created your account, you can start interacting with Google Cloud to create cloud resources such as Cloud Run services, blob storage, and virtual machines.

There are three ways to interact with Google Cloud: the command-line interface gcloud, the web console at console.cloud.google.com, and the Cloud Console mobile app (Figure 2-1).

The web interface is a great way to get to know a product. Most products feature polished getting started wizards that guide you through creating your first resources. I like to stay away from the graphical interface for tasks I perform often. The gcloud command-line interface offers a good user experience, with helpful suggestions if you mistype a command. Most listings in this book use gcloud, not the web console.

The third client is the official Cloud Console mobile app. Its main use cases are monitoring and quick resource and user management. Personally, I do not use it often.

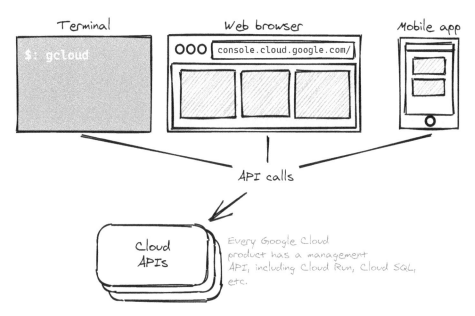

Figure 2-1. Interacting with Google Cloud to manage cloud resources

Google Cloud Projects

On Google Cloud, a *project* is how you organize your applications. Every cloud resource you create—such as a Cloud Run service, a virtual machine, or an access policy—has to belong to a single project. Resources in the same project are aware of one another and can communicate, but resources in different projects are isolated from one another.

Installing and Authenticating the SDK

The first step after creating your account is to install the SDK (*https:// cloud.google.com/sdk*). Make sure to authenticate your local install:

```
gcloud init
```

If you've worked with Google Cloud before, verify that you have the project you want to use for this book set as the default (this should output the project ID you selected):

```
gcloud config get-value project
```

If it isn't set, set it as follows ([PROJECT-ID] stands in for the project you want to use):

```
$: gcloud config set project [PROJECT-ID]
Updated property [core/project].
```

If you're not sure what project ID to use, you can find the projects you have created using:

```
gcloud projects list
```

Installing Beta Components

The gcloud SDK provides access to features that are still in beta using the `gcloud beta` command, which you need to install separately:

```
gcloud components install beta
```

When a product or feature is still in beta, it's a completed product that is still being tested, so it might see some changes. I'm telling you to install the beta component because a few of the features I discuss in the book are still in beta as I write this in October 2020. By the time you read this, they will likely be generally available, but I don't want to take chances and set you up with command listings that don't work.

Deploying Your First Service

I've created a sample container image for you to explore Cloud Run: it contains an app that displays metadata about the requests it gets, the instance it runs on, and additional data it collects from its environment.

A *container image* is a self-contained package with your application and everything it needs to run. If you run a container image, that's called a *container*. Cloud Run expects your container to listen for incoming requests on port 8080, running an HTTP server. The port number 8080 is a default you can override when you deploy the container.

You don't need to become a container expert to make the most of Cloud Run. However, you will make the most of Cloud Run if you understand how they really work, which is why I cover containers from first principles in Chapter 3.

Deploying the Sample Container

When you deploy a container image to Cloud Run for the first time, it creates a service for you. A service automatically gets a unique HTTPS endpoint (more about that later).

If requests come in, Cloud Run starts your container to handle them. It adds more instances of your container if needed to handle all incoming requests, automatically scaling up and down.[1]

---

1 Scaling can be horizontal (adding instances) or vertical (more resources per instance). I refer to horizontal scaling as "scaling up and down" because I think the more correct "scaling in and out" is confusing.

First, you need to enable Cloud Run in your project (you only need to do this once per project):

```
gcloud services enable run.googleapis.com
```

Go ahead and deploy the container. If the next command prompts you to pick a version of the Cloud Run platform, choose "fully-managed." It will ask for a region—pick one that looks geographically close to you (I will explain what a region is in the next section):

```
$: gcloud run deploy hello \
--image gcr.io/cloud-run-book/inspect \
--allow-unauthenticated
Deploying container to Cloud Run service [hello] in project [YOUR-PROJECT] region
[europe-west1]
✓ Deploying... Done.
  ✓ Creating Revision...
  ✓ Routing traffic...
Done.
Service [hello] revision [hello-00001-sav] has been deployed and is serving 100
  percent
of traffic at https://hello-xxxxxx-ew.a.run.app
```

The command deploys your first Cloud Run service, called "hello." It outputs an HTTPS URL. If you open it, you will see my "inspect" program. It shows you metadata: the environment variables of the server, the request headers, and other parameters it gathers from its surroundings.

The `--allow-unauthenticated` flag in the deploy command ensures you can access the URL without passing an authentication header. (I will tell you more about access management in Chapter 6.)

The `--image` flag points to my container image that is stored in a public container registry on Google Cloud so that you can use it. You use a *container registry* to store and distribute container images. In the next chapter, I'll show you how you can push—that is, upload—your own image to Google Cloud's Artifact Registry and deploy the image using Cloud Run.

Region

When you deployed the container, you were prompted to select a region from a list. Every region corresponds to a physical datacenter that is run by Google Cloud. These regions are distributed all over the world (currently excluding mainland China, Russia, and all of Africa). The regions are connected with one another. Google is the largest owner and investor in submarine cable networks globally. This means if you send traffic from one region to another, you'll actually save time if you travel over Google's network instead of over the public internet.

There are regions that don't offer all Google Cloud services. As of October 2020, Cloud Run was still rolling out to all regions. Use the currentlist of available services (*https://cloud.google.com/about/locations*) per region to figure out a good region for you to use. The region in which you choose to deploy your Cloud Run service influences your experience in terms of latency. You probably don't want to pick a region on another continent (unless that's where most of your users are).

I picked Belgium (*europe-west1*) because it is a complete region, and it is close to the Netherlands, where I live. If you are US-based, South Carolina (*us-east1*) or Iowa (*us-central1*) are great regions with a lot of available services.

You can set a default region to avoid the region prompt in the future:

```
gcloud config set run/region us-central1
```

Structure of the HTTPS Endpoint

Let's take a quick look at the URL of the service. You can find the service name, a hash, and the region identifier in the URL:

```
https:// hello  -  rwrmxiaqmq  -    ew    .a.run.app
https:// [name] - [project hash] - [region hash] .a.run.app
```

The *name* is the service name you specify when you deploy (potentially truncated if the name you specified is too long). The *region hash* is a short hash of the region. If your region is *europe-west1*, the short hash is *ew*. Finally, the *project hash* is a hash of your Google Cloud project ID, which is globally unique.[2]

Viewing Your Service in the Web Console

I want to point you in the right direction to configure your service using the web console. Open Google Cloud Platform (*https://oreil.ly/fKKz_*) and make sure to select the correct project; there is a drop-down menu in the blue bar at the top.

Start with selecting the service you've just deployed, called "hello." This brings you to the detail page (Figure 2-2). There are various tabs to explore.

The "Logs" tab is the easiest way to view the logs of your container as they are written. As of September 2020, there is no convenient way to read Cloud Run logs from your terminal, but I have a strong suspicion that this will change soon. On Google Cloud, a product called Cloud Logging handles logging for all cloud resources in a project. (In Chapter 9, I'll explore logging in more depth.)

---

2 There is a small possibility that the project hash is different for different Cloud Run regions in the same project.

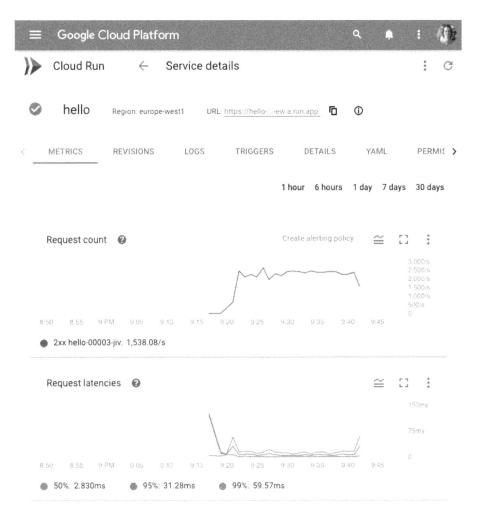

Figure 2-2. Detail page of the `hello` *service*

Deploying a New Version

I've made multiple versions of my program available. The current version you've just deployed is called Emolga, and you can upgrade to another version, called Togepi. The functionality of the app doesn't change between those two versions—the only change is the version name. When you open the *run.app* URL, the app clearly states the currently deployed version.

To change the container image to the new version, use the `update` command:

```
gcloud run services update hello \
  --image gcr.io/cloud-run-book/inspect:togepi
```

When the `update` command finishes and you open the URL again, the version shows as "Togepi." My version names are a bit silly; I often use Pokémon names because there is an ample supply of names, they are easy to pronounce and remember, and they don't carry associations to unrelated concepts (at least for me).

Revision

You use the `update` command to make changes to service configuration, and every change prompts Cloud Run to create a new revision. A *revision* represents a deployment of your service (Figure 2-3).

Every revision has an immutable copy of the service configuration. The configuration is not limited to just the container image, like in the example in the previous section. This is what the configuration includes:

- The full contents of the container image
- Container configuration: arguments, overriding the default program, and environment variables
- Serving configuration, including request timeouts and the default port
- Resource limits: CPU and memory allocation
- Scaling boundaries: minimum and maximum instances
- Platform configuration: service identity and attached resources (network, database)

The default behavior of Cloud Run is to send all traffic to the latest revision as soon as it becomes available, but you can change that behavior to perform a gradual rollout, or deploy a new revision and test it on a separate URL before you switch production traffic over. Take a look at Figure 2-3 for a conceptual model.

You can list the revisions Cloud Run has created for you so far:

```
$: gcloud run revisions list --service hello
    REVISION            ACTIVE  SERVICE      DEPLOYED
 ✓  hello-00002-sif     yes     hello        2020-09-11 08:52:37 UTC
 ✓  hello-00001-vib             hello        2020-09-11 08:51:50 UTC
```

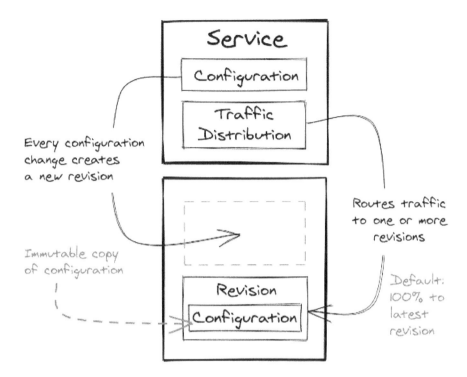

Figure 2-3. *A service manages configuration and traffic distribution*

Revisions are kept unless you delete them, which means you can switch back to an earlier revision with one command. Cloud Run starts to autodelete the oldest revisions once you have more than a thousand revisions, so you can just leave them if you like.

In this example, we roll back 100% of traffic to the first version you deployed, Emolga (make sure to replace `hello-00001-vib` with your first revision name):

```
gcloud run services update-traffic hello \
  --to-revisions hello-00001-vib=100
```

You can also tag revisions (label them) to support more advanced deployment scenarios. For instance, you can choose to *not* send all traffic to the latest revision by default and perform all traffic updates manually.

If you then point a tag to the latest revision, you'll always have a URL available where you can view the latest version in production, before you actually move production traffic to it.

Understanding Cloud Run

Now that you've seen how to perform deployments with Cloud Run, I want to take you on a tour of the internals of Cloud Run. Developing a deep understanding of the platform will help you build more scalable and reliable applications.

Container Life Cycle

Let's start with the container life cycle (Figure 2-4). If you create a new revision, Cloud Run pulls the container image and starts the container. Cloud Run keeps a copy of the image cached so it can be materialized very quickly when a new container needs to start.

As soon as the new container begins listening on port 8080 (a default setting you can override per revision), Cloud Run starts to forward requests: the platform makes sure to handle all incoming requests and adds additional containers if necessary (scaling up). If Cloud Run scales down, it stops sending requests to a container. When that happens, the CPU is throttled.

There are two things that can happen to a container that is not handling requests: Cloud Run can decide to use it again to handle an increase in traffic or shut it down.

The shutdown starts with Cloud Run sending a SIGTERM signal and removing the throttling of the CPU. After a short grace period, the container is shut down permanently. There is no way you can influence which containers will be shut down or kept.

The SIGTERM signal is a warning that says to a process: "Heads up, I am stopping you soon." You can catch the signal from your application. This is a good time to clean up. You'll get 10 seconds to shut down. You should close database connections and flush buffers programmatically. For example, if you use a monitoring agent that collects metrics, it might send the metrics in batches to the monitoring system and hold the current batch in a local buffer. If you don't flush (transmit) the buffer before shutdown, you'll lose the last data points.

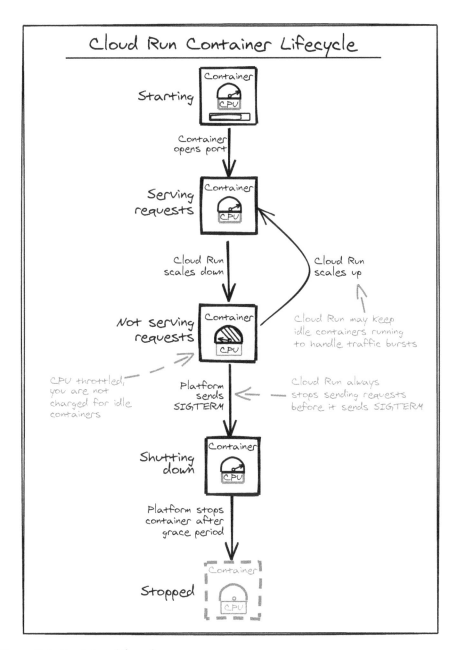

Figure 2-4. Container life cycle

CPU Throttling

Cloud Run guarantees full availability of the CPU as long as a container is handling HTTP requests. If a container is not handling requests, your container will still get a slice of CPU time every now and then, but it's not enough to do meaningful work.

You are only paying for resources while a container is actively handling requests, so it makes sense that Cloud Run applies throttling. If it didn't, you would have a great way to get free CPU time on Google Cloud.

Task Scheduling and Throttling

A common pattern is to schedule work to be performed immediately after the HTTP request is returned, but this is not reliable on Cloud Run because of CPU throttling.

Here's a concrete example: you have an endpoint that allows the user to upload a profile picture. The user uploads a full-resolution picture and you want to process it; you need to scale, crop, and recompress the image before you upload it to your database. However, the user doesn't necessarily need to wait on the processing. On a traditional server, you can return a response to the user as soon as you receive the upload and spawn a background thread to do the processing. On Cloud Run, because of throttling, this background thread might never complete.

This issue is most visible when your application is under low load or when scaling down—throttling happens only if a container handles no other requests. In this case, background work will not complete.

Another issue can manifest if your background task uses a lot of CPU. That will reduce the capacity of the container to handle other requests at the same time, leading to HTTP 503 errors when scaling up. (More about that in the next section.)

There are ways to do reliable task scheduling; Chapter 7 explores the options.

Load Balancer and Autoscaler

On Cloud Run, the load balancer[3] and autoscaler work together to make sure there are enough containers available to handle all incoming requests. I've visualized how this works in Figure 2-5.

The *load balancer* receives incoming requests to a service and forwards them to available containers. If no containers are available to handle the request, the load balancer holds the request temporarily in the (service-level) request buffer until the autoscaler makes a new container available. The autoscaler decides to add and remove

---

3 If you're already familiar with Google Cloud, I'm referring to an internal component of Cloud Run, not to the Global Load Balancer (GLB).

containers. It aims to avoid service-level request buffering and tries to maximize the utilization of containers.

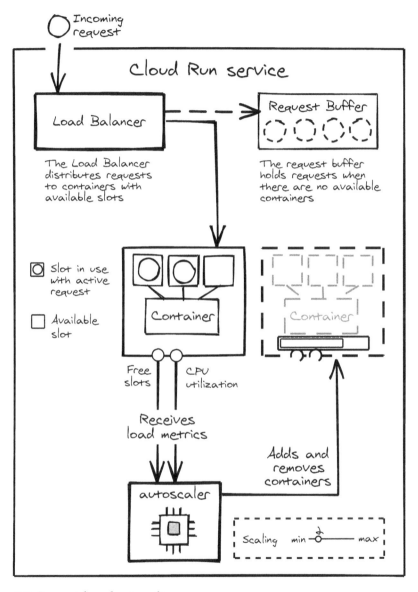

Figure 2-5. Request-based autoscaling

Concurrent Request Limit

The load balancer distributes incoming requests over the available containers. It uses a concurrent request limit to decide if a container can accept another request. You can visualize this limit as a number of available request slots per container—while a request is being handled by the container, it occupies a slot. If there are no slots available on a container, the load balancer will not send additional requests. The number of slots per container is a setting called *concurrency*.

If there are no free request slots available on any container, an incoming request is temporarily held in the request buffer until a slot frees up. If there are no (zero) containers available, the request waits until a new container is ready.

The next example deploys a service with a concurrency level of 1. Every container will have only one request slot available, which means every request will have exclusive access to the container. This is great for CPU-intensive workloads:

```
gcloud run deploy hello \
  --image [IMAGE-URL] \
  --concurrency 1
```

A concurrency level of 1 is also useful if your application is not thread safe and can handle only one request at the same time.

Autoscaler

The autoscaler collects metrics from the containers to determine the number of containers that should be available to handle requests. It acts on the number of available request slots; if that number runs low, it starts a new container (replica) to avoid request buffering.

Additionally, the autoscaler looks at the CPU utilization of the containers. If CPU usage on the containers is high, the autoscaler can decide to add a container even when there are still enough request slots available. This is a situation you generally want to avoid.

The autoscaler will keep adding containers if necessary until it reaches the maximum limit. By default, this is set to a thousand containers. You can decrease or increase the limit. When Cloud Run reaches the maximum limit, it will start returning requests with the HTTP 429 error status. It is important to realize that Cloud Run itself is limited by the available capacity in its datacenter. If you want to be able to use more than the maximum of a thousand containers, you need to apply for a quota increase. This will give you the opportunity to share your desired capacity with the Google Cloud team, who will ensure the datacenter has enough capacity for your needs.

Tuning the Concurrency Setting

As of November 2020, the default concurrency is 250, and this default is most likely too high for your application. Most applications run out of CPU before they manage to handle 250 concurrent requests, especially if they are using a heftier runtime such as Python. Other types of applications can handle a lot more than 250 connections using little CPU if they are primarily waiting on data from downstream systems. You shouldn't be concerned too much about the concurrency setting—the autoscaler also acts on CPU usage.

If you really care about handling traffic bursts with rapid scaling, it is beneficial if your concurrency setting is just right. In this case, you want the autoscaler to act on request slots only and never on high CPU, as it is a slower signal to scale on.

Cold Starts

If you've just deployed a new container image and the first request comes in, it waits in the request buffer until your container opens port 8080. This is commonly called a *cold start*. It happens when you've just created a new revision. It can also occur when your service does not receive traffic for a while.

Cold starts can also happen during scale-up, but they are less likely: a request in the request buffer is only assigned to a container at the very last moment. Even while waiting for a new container, a request slot on an existing container might become available.

The autoscaler might also decide to proactively keep a small pool of throttled containers ready to handle request bursts. You are not paying for a throttled container since it is not handling requests. Waking a container can happen instantaneously, while starting a new one takes more time depending on how fast your container is ready for requests.

If you want to be sure there is always a container available for requests, you can set minimum instances: a setting that tells the autoscaler to always keep a certain number of containers ready.

Disposable Containers

Containers can be rebooted, become unhealthy, or disappear due to scaling. You should treat them as disposable. This means you always need to store data you don't want to lose in a downstream system like a database.

This doesn't mean you can't use the filesystem or memory of a container. You do, however, need to be careful and think about what happens when the container disappears and takes the data with it.

Here are concrete examples of data you can save on a disposable container (in-memory or on the filesystem):

- Cache data that can be easily rebuilt
- Temporary data that you store only while handling a request (and throw away before you return the request)
- Templates that are compiled on the fly
- Database connections

In-Memory Filesystem

The disposable containers in Cloud Run have a small disk. You can write to the disk, but if you are tempted to download a big data file to your container, be aware that the filesystem is in memory. This means that every byte you write will end up using memory (the maximum was 4 GB as of October 2020). If you try to write over 4 GB, your container is forced to stop as soon as it exceeds the memory limit. This is an event you generally want to avoid, as you'll get no chance to clean up or stop in-flight requests.

Ready for Requests

Cloud Run sends requests to a container as soon as it accepts new connections on port 8080. This behavior might cause issues for stacks that open a port before they are ready to handle requests. An example is the combination of NGINX and PHP-FPM: NGINX opens the port before PHP can handle the requests. There is no way to change how Cloud Run checks if the container is ready. However, in this example you could decide to use Apache instead of NGINX—that stack that doesn't suffer from the same problem.

There is one little hidden surprise: if a container on Cloud Run sends more than 20 *consecutive* responses with HTTP status 5xx (500 to 599), the container is taken out of service and replaced.

Cloud Run Key Points

Has reading this put a damper on your initial enthusiasm? Some things that are very easy to do in a serverful environment are different on Cloud Run, like handling large file uploads or running background tasks. That can feel restrictive, especially if you have a substantial background in serverful programming.

I am very excited about the fully managed Cloud Run platform. Its characteristics provide an environment that gently pushes you to build applications that will not go down under load or become slow and unattractive for your users. The limitations serve as guardrails that help you build applications that are highly scalable and reliable, just like the platform itself.

Here are the key things to remember about Cloud Run:

- It lets you invoke your container on an HTTPS endpoint.
- It automatically adds and removes instances of your container, scaling up and down to handle all requests.
- You can only perform meaningful work *while handling* an HTTP request—Cloud Run will throttle the CPU of containers that are not handling requests.
- While you can save a limited amount of data on disk and in memory, you should only use it for transient data that can be easily rebuilt.
- If you carefully tune the concurrent request limit, you can unlock better performance.

Choosing a Serverless Compute Product on Google Cloud

This book teaches you how to build applications with Cloud Run because it is container based and offers unparalleled portability on top of a cost model that is friendly for concurrent workloads. However, there are other options, such as Cloud Functions or App Engine. I want to highlight the trade-offs involved in deciding which option is good for your use case.

Cloud Functions: Glue Code

Cloud Functions is very similar to Cloud Run, but it offers source-based deploys instead. You write your code, state the dependencies, and use a gcloud command to deploy it. All the packaging is handled by the product itself.

At runtime, your code will plug into the Cloud Functions language-specific runtime framework. Essentially, you export a method or function that will be called by this framework. The available runtimes include Node.js, Java, Python, and Go.

The product excels at being the glue that connects and extends other Google Cloud services. Here are a few examples:

- When a file is uploaded to a Cloud Storage bucket, it triggers a Cloud Function to read the file metadata and save it in a database.
- A function runs a virus scan on user-uploaded files.
- A function automatically creates tickets in your support system when monitoring alarms are triggered.

- Every day, at the end of the working day, a scheduled Cloud Function scales down all clusters in your development environment.
- A function cleans up old data periodically.

Cloud Functions is not meant to serve highly concurrent workloads, such as web applications or APIs. For example, Cloud Functions does not support traffic splitting or easy revision management to roll back versions, and a Cloud Function handles only one endpoint. A Cloud Function also uses one container exclusively to handle a single request. This is fine for workloads that compute a lot (CPU), but it wastes resources for IO-intensive workloads.

App Engine: Platform as a Service

App Engine is the serverless application platform that predates Google Cloud. If you use one of the standard runtimes, you are actually using the *same* underlying platform that powers Cloud Functions and Cloud Run. In fact, if you want to prototype an application quickly and you want to use one of the mature web frameworks out there, App Engine will get you to production fast. Some notable implementations include Snapchat and Pokémon Go.

One thing that makes App Engine less attractive is that it carries the weight of a decade of product development. This means some features are in there because they have been there for a long time, not necessarily because they are still relevant today. This is particularly apparent if you dive into the different runtimes. There are three distinctly different classes of runtimes to choose from. There is a Standard version and a Flexible version, and Standard offers a first-generation and a second-generation runtime. The Standard version runs on the same platform as Cloud Run and Cloud Functions, whereas Flexible runs on top of Compute Engine, which results in wildly different scaling characteristics.

On App Engine Flexible, the underlying servers are visible to you, and you can even use SSH to get to them. App Engine Flexible is a popular option if you need features that are available only on Compute Engine but you still want App Engine to manage your servers.

Key Differences

Now that you have learned about Cloud Run, Cloud Functions, and App Engine, how do you actually make a decision? Let's look at the key differences.

The use case for Cloud Functions is very well defined. You can use Cloud Functions to connect and extend existing services. A concrete example is when you want to process images that are uploaded to a Cloud Storage bucket. You use a function to create a thumbnail and call the Vision API to figure out what the picture is about.

If you want to build something that is user facing and looks more like a service, like an API or a web application, you can use either Cloud Run or App Engine. This choice can be harder to make. The crucial differences are between source-based and container-based, and between request-oriented and instance-oriented. Let's look at them one by one.

Source-based versus container-based

App Engine is source-based. Your code runs inside a standard, language-specific runtime. You upload your source code and list your dependencies (binary dependencies excluded). Cloud Run lets you upload a container image with your own runtime, which is supposed to start listening on a port and handle HTTP requests.

I favor a container-based platform over a source-based one. A container provides a very clear division of responsibilities between me, the developer, and the platform it runs on. My responsibility is to start a binary, which opens a port to receive HTTP requests on; the platform runs my container. Using a container-based platform does require me to create a container and start my own HTTP server, but that is a small price to pay for long-term stability and portability.

A benefit of the source-based approach is that the base layers of the underlying instances are automatically patched. The runtime receives minor version updates on deployment, such as Go 1.12.1 to Go 1.12.2, without your intervention. This offers peace of mind and reduces your maintenance responsibilities.

Cloud Run can also be used in a source-based workflow using Google Cloud Build-packs (I dive into that in the next chapter).

Request- versus instance-oriented runtime

Cloud Run is request-oriented: the lifetime of a container is guaranteed only while it is handling a request cycle. On App Engine Standard, you can still use background threads in a meaningful way because throttling does not happen. The same goes for billing: App Engine charges with less granularity for active instances, while Cloud Run charges per request.

App Engine might be a better option for you if you are looking for an easy entry into serverless.

What Will the Future Look Like?

I am fairly certain that Cloud Run is the future of serverless on Google Cloud. Google is traditionally very secretive about its product roadmap and product life cycle. As an outsider, all I can do is speculate. However, there is nothing holding me back from sharing my predictions with you.

After its introduction, Cloud Run was rapidly rolled out to multiple regions, which shows that Google put significant resources behind the development of the platform. Cloud Run has seen solid improvements ever since.

The pricing model of Cloud Run seems to be designed to be cheaper than both App Engine and Cloud Functions for most workloads, which nudges customers to adopt Cloud Run.

With the introduction of the second-generation runtimes on App Engine, the proprietary App Engine SDK was removed and replaced with open source client libraries. Cloud Tasks and Cloud Scheduler, once part of App Engine, are now separate services. This increases the portability of code that runs on App Engine and provides an upgrade path to Cloud Run. With the introduction of Google Cloud Buildpacks, Google made the code that App Engine uses to turn source code into a container image open source.

The story for Cloud Functions is similar. All runtimes have an open source Functions Framework, providing an easy upgrade path to Cloud Run.

I don't think existing customers of App Engine have to worry that their favorite platform will suddenly be discontinued. The proposition caters to unique use cases, and the installed base is simply too big.

Summary

In this chapter, you deployed your first Cloud Run service. Cloud Run is built on open standards and has a container-based runtime environment. It offers good scalability and portability out of the box.

I discussed the characteristics of the Cloud Run runtime and helped you understand how it can influence your application design and how its limitations are like guardrails that help you build scalable and reliable applications. The next chapter will dive into building containers, starting from first principles.

## CHAPTER 3

Building Containers

In Chapter 2, I showed you how to deploy my sample container image on Cloud Run. If you want to deploy your code to Cloud Run, you need to build your code into a container image and push it to Artifact Registry to deploy (Figure 3-1). This chapter will show you how to do that.

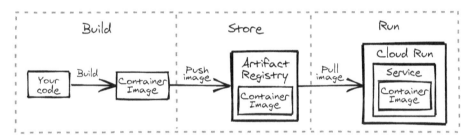

Figure 3-1. The full development workflow

Artifact Registry is a product on Google Cloud that helps you host and distribute container images and other build artifacts such as npm and Maven packages. You'll need to create a repository to store the container images you'll create while working through the book.

I'll start by explaining container technology from first principles. It will be a great introduction if you're just getting started with containers; if you're already an expert, it's a useful review of what you already know.

With the fundamental concepts covered, I'll show you various approaches to turn your source code into a container image. I'll start with Docker, which offers a relatively low-level experience, and show you how to store your local container image in Artifact Registry on Google Cloud.

I will follow up with three alternatives to Docker that require (almost) no configuration. If you've ever struggled to create a small, secure image while trying to learn Docker from scratch (I know I have), you will love this last part.

Finally, I'll demonstrate the various ways you can leverage Cloud Build to build containers on Google Cloud instead of on your local machine. Yes, you read that right: you use Cloud Run to run container images and Cloud Build to build them.

Containers: A Hands-On Exploration

I'll lead you through three examples so you can get some hands-on experience running containers on your local machine and see what using containers with Docker looks like.

First, I'll show you how to run a container with an interactive shell. Second, you'll override the default command and run a different command. Finally, I'll show you how to start my sample container image from Chapter 2 locally.

If you haven't already, install Docker Desktop (*http://docker.com*) on your local machine.

Running an Interactive Shell

As the first example, I want you to run a shell using the "bash" container image. A *container image* is a self-contained bundle of a program and its dependencies, like libraries and static assets—in this example, the bash shell and a few tools.

If you execute the command `docker run -it bash`, Docker pulls (that is, downloads) the container image *docker.io/library/bash* from Docker Hub and starts it. You will be greeted by the bash shell, where you can type commands (the flag `-it` ensures you can use the interactive shell). Here's how it looks when I start the bash container, list the files in the root directory, and request a process list:

```
$: docker run -it bash
Unable to find image 'bash:latest' locally
latest: Pulling from library/bash
df20fa9351a1: Pull complete
59b440fb53b2: Pull complete
6523a82f1e3f: Pull complete
Digest: sha256:21caabbff34a7432be0f88d24f756a96f1e5bbb93703e8a8b34df7c5
Status: Downloaded newer image for bash:latest
bash-5.0# ls /
bin    dev    etc    home   lib    media  mnt    opt    proc   root   run
sbin   srv    sys    tmp    usr    var
bash-5.0# ps -A
PID   USER     TIME   COMMAND
    1 root      0:00 bash
    8 root      0:00 ps -A
```

```
bash-5.0# exit
exit
```

The files you're seeing in the root directory are all part of the container image. You start in a fresh clone of the image every time you run **docker run -it bash**, and you can only see the files in the image.

If you run **ps -A** in the container, it shows just two processes. You can close the shell with the command exit, which will bring you back to your original shell.

To summarize, this is what you've discovered so far: a running container has a private, isolated root filesystem, and it has an isolated namespace to run processes. In a container, you can only see the processes that were started in the container.

Overriding the Default Command

Another way to use a container is to run a one-off program instead of a long-running process like a shell. I'll show you how to run the *ping* program using the same bash container image. You can override the default program (in this case, the shell) using the --entrypoint flag:

```
$: docker run --entrypoint ping bash google.com -c1
PING google.com (172.217.20.78): 56 data bytes
64 bytes from 172.217.20.78: seq=0 ttl=37 time=12.567 ms

--- google.com ping statistics ---
1 packets transmitted, 1 packets received, 0% packet loss
round-trip min/avg/max = 12.567/12.567/12.567 ms
```

In this example, I run the command ping google.com -c1. Notice how the command and the flags are separate—I override the command (ping) with the --entrypoint flag, and the parameters to that command (google.com -c1) go after the name of the container image.

Running a Server

You can also use Docker to run the container image you deployed to Cloud Run in Chapter 2 on your local machine:

```
docker run -p 9000:8080 gcr.io/cloud-run-book/inspect
```

The -p flag tells Docker that requests to a port on your local machine (9000) should be forwarded to a port on the container (8080). If you now open *http://localhost:9000*, you will see the same page you saw earlier on Cloud Run. To stop the container, go back to the terminal and enter **Ctrl-C**.

This shows you that a container has its own network stack that is separate from the network stack of your local machine.

Containers from First Principles

Now that you've had some hands-on experience, let's dig into the fundamentals. This section will help you make sense of what you saw when running the example commands.

If you like to learn by example, feel free to skip ahead to the next section, where I show you how to build a container image.

Inside a Container Image

What's inside a container image? As you learned in the previous section, a *container image* is a self-contained bundle of a program and its dependencies. Figure 3-2 shoows this visually.

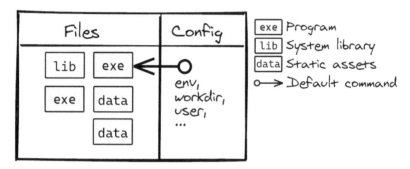

Figure 3-2. Contents of a container image

The files in a container image are programs, system libraries, and static assets. The key point here is that a container image contains one or more programs and all of the files those programs need in order to run.

Static assets can include HTML templates, CSS files, configuration files, images, and source code. *Source code* can be an interpreted language like PHP, Python, or Java-Script. If so, one of the programs will be the runtime you need to run your application, such as Node, Python, or Apache with PHP.

The second part of the container image is the *image configuration*. This points out the program to run when you start the container and the parameters used to execute that program. Those include the working directory, environment variables, and the user ID (the default is to run as root).

If the process opens a file using a relative path, the kernel uses the process *working directory* to figure out the absolute path. *Environment variables* are used to pass configuration to a process. Finally, with the *user ID*, the kernel applies access control (what files the process can read or write to).

You can find additional metadata in the configuration, such as the CPU architecture or the OS for which the image is built.

The Linux Kernel

A container image contains one or more programs. I want to review what happens when you start a program—this will help you understand what happens when you start a container.

A *program* is an executable file, which can be started—that is, turned into a *process*—by the Linux kernel. This means the program is loaded into memory and the kernel schedules CPU time for it to run.

The *kernel* is at the core of the Linux OS. It is the central piece of software that controls access to system resources. It schedules processes, controls networking, manages memory, and provisions a filesystem (Figure 3-3).

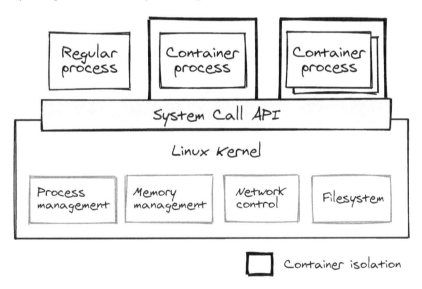

Figure 3-3. The Linux kernel provides container isolation

If you want to learn more about Linux OS fundamentals, I recommend *The Linux Programming Interface* by Michael Kerrisk (No Starch Press, 2010).

Here are a few examples of critical operations only the kernel is allowed to perform:

- Reading data from a file
- Opening a network port
- Starting a new process
- Changing the permissions of a file
- Finding other processes and communicating with them

If a process wants to do something only the kernel can do, it sends a request using the system call API; these requests are commonly called *syscalls*. You normally don't perform syscalls directly, but instead use a higher-level library.

Container Isolation

The kernel controls almost everything a process can do, see, and use. This means the kernel can also isolate a process by changing its perception of its environment (Figure 3-4). For example, the kernel can change the root directory of the process to a folder, making the process think that the entire filesystem is just that single folder.

A process in a container will see a virtual ethernet interface with a local IP. To get traffic to the container, you'll need to tell Docker to forward a port on the local machine.

This is what container technology is about; a *container* is a group of processes that is isolated from other processes on the same host.

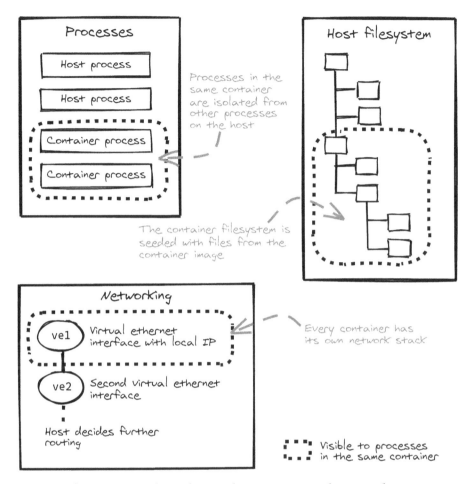

Figure 3-4. *The Linux Kernel can change what a process can do, see, and use*

Starting a Container

When you start a container, Docker works with the kernel to start a program in the container image. It clones the files in the container image, which become the root directory of the new process. The process can only see and interact with *child processes* (processes that it starts). The kernel will make the process believe it has its own hostname and network stack with a local IP address.

If you want to learn more about container fundamentals, I recommend the book *Container Security* by Liz Rice (O'Reilly, 2020). The book helps you build a deep understanding of container technology, which will help you build more secure systems. It also has a lot of references to supplemental material.

Building a Container with Docker

You need a container image to deploy your application to Cloud Run. Since Docker is the ubiquitous container technology, I'll give you a short tour and explain how to build containers with Docker. I'll introduce you to the concepts and show you how to read and understand a Dockerfile.

Docker takes local files (Docker calls this the "build context") and a Dockerfile and turns them into a container image (Figure 3-5). A *Dockerfile* is a list of instructions to build a container image. Docker reads the instructions one by one. I'll first show you a Dockerfile and how to use `docker build`. Be aware that this first example is not production ready; I will improve on it in subsequent sections to make the resulting container image smaller and more secure.

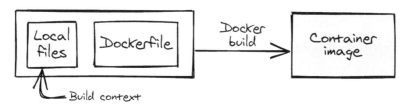

Figure 3-5. Docker turns local files and a Dockerfile into a container image

The next Dockerfile is the recipe to turn a directory with a Go app into a container image. You can find the code on GitHub (*https://oreil.ly/iUGZ3*) if you want to reproduce the examples on your local machine:

```
FROM golang:1.15

# Download dependencies
WORKDIR /src
COPY go.* ./
RUN go mod download

# Compile app
COPY . /src
RUN go build -o /main

ENTRYPOINT ["/main"]
```

Now take a look at what happens when you run `docker build`. Make sure you are in the directory with the cloned repository when you run this command. (I've edited this listing to improve readability; if you run the same statement on your local machine, you will see more output):

```
$: docker build . --tag hello-go -f Dockerfile.simple

Sending build context to Docker daemon  87.04kB

Step 1/7 : FROM golang:1.15
1.15: Pulling from library/golang
Status: Downloaded newer image for golang:1.15

Step 2/7 : WORKDIR /src
 ---> Running in 5aa70e27b4e1
 ---> e490f619a38f

[Edited: Removed stap 3-5]

Step 6/7 : RUN go build -o /main
 ---> Running in 9fd9af1aef59
 ---> 040645f606d3

Step 7/7 : ENTRYPOINT ["/main"]
 ---> Running in a71a9eb00059
 ---> b2ca92c1575c

Successfully built b2ca92c1575c
Successfully tagged hello-go:latest
```

Docker starts by sending the build context (the local directory) to Docker. It then starts to execute the Dockerfile line by line.

Dockerfile Instructions

The first instruction (`FROM`) in the preceding example lists `golang:1.15`. This is an image on Docker Hub. It contains all the tools you need to build Go applications. The next statements (steps 2 through 7) compile the source code to finally set the application as the default command to run when the container starts.

Every instruction in the Dockerfile modifies the container image. You can pull in files from the build context (`COPY`), change image configuration (`ENV`), or actually run a program inside of the image as a container (`RUN`). The instruction `FROM` is special: it overwrites the entire image with another image. In Table 3-1, you can find an overview of all of the instructions used in the example Dockerfile and how they act on the container image.

There are more than six instructions[1] you can use in a Dockerfile, but these cover almost every use case.

Table 3-1. Dockerfile instructions

Instruction	Files	Image configuration
FROM	Overwrites files	Overwrites configuration
COPY	Adds files from the build context (local files) or a named stage to the image	*Not applicable*
RUN	Runs a command in the image and saves the changes made to file	*Not applicable*
WORKDIR	Creates the directory if it doesn't exist	Changes the default working directory
ENV	*Not applicable*	Adds an environment variable
ENTRYPOINT	*Not applicable*	Changes the default command to run

Installing Additional Tooling

In the example, I used tools from the golang image to compile my application. If you want to install additional tooling that is not included in the image, you can. Most container images, like golang, include a package manager. Here's an example of a Dockerfile that installs additional software:

```
FROM debian:bullseye
RUN apt-get update && apt-get install cowsay -y
ENTRYPOINT ["/usr/games/cowsay"]
```

If you copy this listing to a Dockerfile and build an image, you can use it to have a cow repeat what you say:

```
$: docker build --tag cowsay -f Dockerfile
[SNIP]
Successfully tagged cowsay:latest
$: docker run cowsay Hello World
 _____
< Hello World >
 -------------
        \   ^__^
         \  (oo)_____
            (__)\       )\/\
                ||----w |
                ||     ||
```

Of course this is a silly example, but it shows that you can install additional tooling to build your application.

---

1 COPY and ENTRYPOINT have alternatives with different semantics (ADD and CMD, respectively) that can be confusing. As a rule, stick with COPY and ENTRYPOINT.

In this case, I used `apt-get` to install the cowsay program. The `FROM` line of the cowsay example lists the container image *debian,* a Linux distribution. This doesn't mean that you actually run Debian when you use this image. Rather, it means that the image contains the package manager apt-get and a set of packages that are already installed and configured in the image. Similar packages exist for other Linux distributions, including, for example, Ubuntu and CentOS.

The `golang` image is based on Debian, so if I wanted, I could install additional tooling using `apt-get`.

Smaller Is Better When Deploying to Production

I want to make one final, important improvement to the example before this whirlwind tour of building container images with Docker is over. The image you've built is large:

```
$: docker images
REPOSITORY          IMAGE ID        CREATED          SIZE
hello-go            b2ca92c1575c    2 minutes ago    826MB
```

This is because the image is based on the golang container image. It is meant to be used to build your Go app, which means it includes a broad range of tools, including Git, Subversion, cURL, the package manager apt-get I just mentioned, and a lot more.

However, if you deploy a container image to production, smaller is better. Your application generally doesn't need the Git package to be installed in order to run. If you do ship it in your application container, you're transmitting data unnecessarily, making your deployments slower.

Security is an additional reason to have small container images in production that only contain what is needed. In a 2019 study by Snyk (*https://oreil.ly/--7LB*), researchers found that the top-10 most popular base images (such as Debian and golang) each contained 30 or more system libraries with known vulnerabilities. The image for Node topped the chart with over 500 known vulnerabilities. These are serious issues that you often can't actively mitigate because they are in the base image itself.

Creating Small Containers with Distroless

Distroless is a project that can help you build small application images with multistage Dockerfiles. The `FROM` line can be repeated in a Dockerfile. If you repeat it, the next line in the Dockerfile starts fresh with a new image (a new stage), and you can use `COPY` to pull in specific files from the previous image.

This is the same Dockerfile, but with an additional stage to copy just the compiled application into a distroless image:

```
# A named stage: "build"
FROM golang:1.15 AS build

WORKDIR /go/src/app
COPY go.* /go/src/app/
RUN go mod download

COPY . /go/src/app
RUN go build -o /go/bin/app

# A new stage: "run"
FROM gcr.io/distroless/base-debian10:nonroot AS run

# Copy the binary from stage build
COPY --from=build /go/bin/app /

ENTRYPOINT ["/app"]
```

If you build the image again and compare the sizes of both, you can see that the container is now almost 800 MB smaller:

```
$: docker build . --tag hello-go-multistage -f Dockerfile
[SNIP]
Successfully tagged hello-go-multistage:latest
$: docker images
REPOSITORY            IMAGE ID       CREATED          SIZE
hello-go-multistage   7d7ba942334f   3 seconds ago    26.7MB
hello-go              b2ca92c1575c   7 minutes ago    826MB
```

The Distroless project (*https://oreil.ly/4Dxlf*) aims to deliver a selection of container images that contain just enough dependencies to run an application, and nothing more. You won't find any tooling: no shell, no package manager, and almost no system libraries.

There are various flavors of distroless containers, optimized for different use cases. The one I use in this example contains just a few system libraries from Debian 10. There are also distroless images available for other application runtimes, including Node.js, Java, and Python. You can find examples in the Distroless repository.

Artifact Registry

Artifact Registry is a product on Google Cloud that helps you host and distribute container images. (You might be familiar with the product Container Registry; Artifact Registry is the successor to Container Registry and provides more features.) If you want to deploy a container image on Cloud Run, you'll need to upload the container image to Artifact Registry first, as Cloud Run can only pull container images from there.

In this section, I'll show you how to create a repository on Artifact Registry where you'll store the container images you'll build while working through this book. When that's done, you'll build, tag, and push (upload) the container image to the repository.

First, you need to enable Artifact Registry in your project:

```
gcloud services enable artifactregistry.googleapis.com
```

Before you can push container images, you need to create a repository. I will call it cloud-run-book:

```
gcloud artifacts repositories create \
  --location us \
  --repository-format docker \
  cloud-run-book
```

Artifact Registry is a regional product with multiregion support: you can choose between the US, Asia, and Europe. In this listing, I use the multiregion "us." You can choose a different region, but remember to use that region in all other snippets in this book.

Building and Tagging the Container Image

Before you can push the image, you'll need to build and tag it with the right image URL. Go back to the directory where you cloned the repository (*https://oreil.ly/ J4NW7*).

Your Google Cloud Project name is part of the URL. Set up another environment variable with your project ID:

```
PROJECT=$(gcloud config get-value project)
```

You can now construct the image URL in another environment variable:

```
IMAGE=us-docker.pkg.dev/$PROJECT/cloud-run-book/hello
```

Finally, you need to build and tag the container image. Make sure you are in the directory with the source and run docker build:

```
docker build . -t $IMAGE -f Dockerfile
```

You now have the container image with the correct URL, but it's still stored on your local machine (run docker images to list all local images).

Authenticating and Pushing the Container Image

To let Docker push the local image to Artifact Registry, you need to set up credentials:

```
gcloud auth configure-docker us-docker.pkg.dev
```

You can now push the image to Artifact Registry:

```
docker push $IMAGE
```

The next step—if you want—is to deploy the image to Cloud Run:

```
gcloud run deploy hello-world \
  --image $IMAGE \
  --allow-unauthenticated
```

Building a Container Without a Dockerfile

You might feel a bit overwhelmed, especially if this is your first experience with container technology. If you feel like that, you are not alone—building containers with a Dockerfile can be pretty complicated. Here are a few questions sampled from Stack Overflow, the question-and-answer site for developers:

- Setting WORKDIR doesn't seem to have an effect?
- What is the difference between COPY and ADD?
- Why are those two lines different: "CMD npm start" and CMD ["npm", "start"]
- Why is having a single line with just "RUN apt-get update" considered a bad practice?
- What is the best base-image to use for a Python web app?
- How to build a Docker container for a Java application?
- My image is 2.23 Gb, how do I reduce the size?

Stack Overflow had around 84,000 questions tagged with "docker" when I checked in August 2020. This is why I want to show you three additional ways—that *don't* involve writing a Dockerfile—to turn your application source code into a container image.

A container image is basically an archive with files and configuration. You don't need Docker to create a container image.

I cover three different approaches in this section. First, I look at ko, which is a tool used to create a container image with a Go app. Second, I explain Jib (for Java containers), and finally, I take a look at Google Cloud Buildpacks.

Go Containers with ko

ko is a tool that helps you build Go apps and deploy them to Kubernetes (a popular open source container orchestration platform). It also supports a workflow that is helpful if you are deploying to Cloud Run. I will illustrate this with the same sample application I used when I demonstrated docker build. If you haven't already, clone the repository (*https://oreil.ly/29b4v*). There are a few Dockerfiles there, but you will not use them—you're using ko instead. This is what ko handles for you:

1. Statically compiles the Go app

2. Puts the binary in a distroless container image

3. Pushes the container image to Artifact Registry

If you run into trouble following my instructions, you can find up-to-date documentation in the project's repository on GitHub (*https://oreil.ly/ztmav*).

Let's start with the prerequisites: install ko and set up the link to Artifact Registry:

```
GO111MODULE=on go get github.com/google/ko/cmd/ko
```

You need to tell ko where to push images to using the KO_DOCKER_REPO[2] environment variable. This is how you point it to the repository you created in the previous section (make sure to update the region):

```
PROJECT=$(gcloud config get-value project)
export KO_DOCKER_REPO=us-docker.pkg.dev/$PROJECT/cloud-run-book
```

With all the prerequisites out of the way, you can get started. Make sure you are in the directory with the hello-docker-go repository when you run this:

```
ko publish -P github.com/wietsevenema/hello-docker-go
```

The publish command compiles the Go app, packages it into a container image, and publishes the image to Artifact Registry. The github.com URL is the package import path in the local directory—you're not downloading the source again.

The final line of output from the publish command is the image URL—it's the value of KO_DOCKER_REPO with the package import path appended. You can copy and paste this (rather long) image URL into a gcloud command to deploy the image, but there is a better way: ko can work with a YAML configuration file.

---

2 This variable name, KO_DOCKER_REPO (Docker repository), is confusing, because it can point to any container registry—it's not limited to Docker.

Cloud Run has a `replace` command, which takes a YAML configuration of service. You can view the YAML configuration of the `hello-world` service you deployed earlier in this chapter with this command:

```
gcloud run services describe hello-world --format yaml
```

The output is rather verbose, but you don't need to specify all the defaults and runtime status information. Take a look at the example *service.yml* in the repository:

```
apiVersion: serving.knative.dev/v1
kind: Service
metadata:
 name: hello-ko
spec:
 template:
   spec:
     containers:
     - image: ko://github.com/wietsevenema/hello-docker-go
```

This YAML file describes a service named `hello-ko`. The format of the YAML file is specified by the Knative Serving API specification (*https://oreil.ly/pJIoS*). I will dive deeper into Knative in Chapter 10.

The *service.yml* file refers to the container image using ko://*[package import path]*. That's not a valid container image URI. The idea is that ko replaces this value on the fly. The `ko resolve` command creates a new container image and outputs the YAML configuration with the new container image URI. You can pipe the YAML output through to the `replace` command:

```
ko resolve -f service.yml | gcloud beta run services replace -
```

The `replace` command takes the YAML output from ko (that's what the trailing dash means) and updates the service. The `replace` command does not have a flag, `--allow-unauthenticated`, to allow public access. This is how you add the access policy (you only need to do this once for every service):

```
gcloud run services add-iam-policy-binding hello-ko \
  --member=allUsers \
  --role=roles/run.invoker
```

The `replace` command is authoritative, which means it replaces the entire service configuration with the settings in *service.yml* except for the identity and access management (IAM) policy bindings, which are managed separately.

If I am trying to figure out how to add a setting to the YAML file, I usually make the change using gcloud as I would normally, run `gcloud run services` (like I showed earlier) to learn the right way to express the setting, and update the *service.yml* file.

You'll see more examples of service YAML files in Chapter 10 when I explore Knative Serving.

Java Containers with Jib

Similar to ko, Jib (*https://oreil.ly/WAcvl*) offers developers an integrated experience for packaging their app into a container image. Jib integrates with the two popular build tools in the Java ecosystem: Maven and Gradle. If you have an existing Java project with a `main` class, the only thing needed to containerize your app is to add the Jib plug-in to your `pom.xml` or `build.gradle` files, and you are ready to build a container.

If you add the plug-in, building a container is as simple as typing `mvn compile jib:dockerBuild`. The resulting container is built on top of the Java Distroless container.

If you build a Java container with a Dockerfile, it is common to use the `openjdk` container image, which packages the OpenJDK Java Virtual Machine (JVM). The image with OpenJDK 11 is 627 MB, which is pretty large. The distroless container with exactly the same OpenJDK 11 JVM is 197 MB.

In the past, I worked on Spring-based Java projects where it took more than 10 minutes to redeploy an application on a laptop. This was so common that a healthy ecosystem of vendor products existed to help developers work around the long redeploys by "hot-swapping" code when editing it.

The Java community is still going strong today, and a lot of progress has been made since then. You can build Java-based container images that are small and start in milliseconds. All across the stack, from JVMs to application frameworks, the state of the art is advancing. A project from Oracle, GraalVM (*https://oreil.ly/IMvNn*), allows you to create standalone native binaries from your Java source code. However, GraalVM can break existing frameworks and libraries. I suggest you explore Micronaut for GraalVM (*https://oreil.ly/CE4BC*) or Quarkus (*https://quarkus.io*) to get started with the new-and-improved Java.

I compiled a "Hello World" app with Micronaut and can confirm that it starts in milliseconds and the container image weighs 75 MB.

Cloud Native Buildpacks

Buildpacks turn source code into a container image, just like Jib and ko. The difference is that Buildpacks are standardized—anyone can create a Buildpack to turn any source code into a container image.

To use a Buildpack, start by installing (*https://oreil.ly/1z8Fw*) `pack` (*https://oreil.ly/OaMqV*), the command-line tool. If you have that installed and ready to go, open the directory where you cloned the repository (*https://oreil.ly/29b4v*) you worked with earlier in this chapter.

Now let's locally build a container image from the source code with `pack`. It will take a while to complete the first time because it needs to download dependencies:

```
pack build --builder gcr.io/buildpacks/builder:v1 hello-buildpack
```

This command builds a container image called *hello-buildpack*. Start the container image, and then open *http://localhost:9000* to view the app:

```
docker run -p 9000:8080 hello-buildpack
```

I specified a builder when I ran `pack`. A *builder* contains a list of Buildpacks, each specific to a language runtime (such as Go, Node.js, or Python). Because you are running it in a directory with Go sources, the Go Buildpack activates. Every Buildpack can detect whether it can process the source code—the Node.js Buildpack might look for a *package.json* file, and the Go Buildpack can look for a *go.mod* file.

Multiple vendors have created builders that work with `pack`, including Heroku, VMware, and Google. Supported languages for the Google Cloud Buildpacks (*https://oreil.ly/0sd3g*) include Go, Node.js, Python, Java, and .NET Core.

If you use App Engine or Cloud Functions, the source-based serverless alternatives to Cloud Run, these exact Buildpacks process your source code to turn it into a container image.

Cloud Build

I've shown you four different ways to build a container image on your local machine. Google Cloud also offers a service to build container images remotely on Google Cloud: Cloud Build.

I think Cloud Build is the best-kept secret on Google Cloud because it is surprisingly simple and versatile. It can do much more than just build container images (I'll show you later).

As a first step, enable Cloud Build on your project:

```
gcloud services enable cloudbuild.googleapis.com
```

Remote Docker Build

The simplest way to use Cloud Build is as a "remote docker build." To give an example of how that would fit into your workflow, I want to show you how to deploy to Cloud Run the example application I used to explain docker build.

Go back to the directory where you cloned the repository (*https://oreil.ly/29b4v*). Now use Cloud Build to build the image and push it to Artifact Registry:

```
PROJECT=$(gcloud config get-value project)
REPO=us-docker.pkg.dev/$PROJECT/cloud-run-book

gcloud builds submit --tag $REPO/hello-cloud-build
```

This command first sends your local directory to Cloud Build, and then executes docker build using a virtual machine on Google Cloud. The resulting container image is then sent to Container Registry, which means you can deploy it like this:

```
gcloud run deploy hello-cloud-build \
  --image $REPO/hello-cloud-build \
  --allow-unauthenticated
```

Advanced Builds

I've shown you a very concrete and simple example of Cloud Build, but you can also use it for more complex workflows. I've illustrated the essence of Cloud Build in Figure 3-6.

When you submit a build to Cloud Build, it uploads your source code to a virtual machine, and then lets you execute arbitrary programs consecutively[3] on a shared directory, */workspace*, with your source code in it.

The *cloudbuild.yaml* file configures the build. Every step references a container image that contains the program you want to run.

---

3 Steps that are not dependent on one another can be set to execute in parallel.

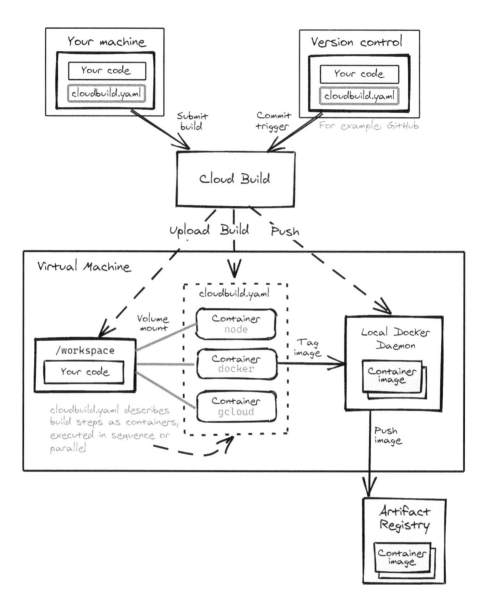

Figure 3-6. Understanding Cloud Build

For example, if you want to run `npm test` to run unit tests, you would add this step to the build configuration (see Example 3-1).

Example 3-1. A build step in cloudbuild.yaml that runs `npm test` on your workspace

```
- name: 'node'      ❶
  entrypoint: 'npm'  ❷
  args: ['test']     ❸
```

❶ The container image you want to use (*node*)

❷ The program you want to start in the container image (`npm`)

❸ The arguments to the program (`test`)

Here are some examples of steps you can put in a *cloudbuild.yaml* file:

- Install dependencies
- Run static code analysis–style checks, detect common error patterns
- Run unit tests
- Compile or package your application sources
- Package the binary and other assets into a container image
- Run component tests on the container image
- Deploy the container to Cloud Run

If one of the steps fails, then execution stops and Cloud Build does not submit the container image to the registry.

Running Arbitrary Programs

You don't *need* to submit a container image at the end of the build. You can execute any program you like, with a timeout of 24 hours, which makes it a great place to run long administrative tasks that need to run to completion (such as database migrations).

Connecting with Version Control

You're not limited to using Cloud Build from your local machine. You can connect Cloud Build with version control—for example, GitHub. This way, you can set up triggers and run a build whenever a commit is pushed to your source code repository. You're not limited to building a container image—you can even drive your deployments from Cloud Build.

If you want to quickly set up a workflow that builds and deploys every commit to Cloud Run, you can find a graphical wizard in the Cloud Run web console that does exactly that.

Shutting Down

You've created several Cloud Run services in this chapter. If you want to avoid being charged, you should not send requests to them; you can keep the services.

If that worries you, you can delete them. List all Cloud Run services:

```
gcloud run services list
```

Then delete the services in question:

```
gcloud run services delete SERVICE
```

Summary

Cloud Run is a container platform. In this chapter, you learned different approaches to turn your source code into a container. Docker—which is ubiquitous—provides a low-level approach to creating containers. I covered just enough ground to make sure you can interpret a Dockerfile.

I made a case for tooling that uses a higher level of abstraction to build containers more specific to the application you're trying to package. The tool ko builds and packages Go applications. You discovered a YAML-based workflow that lets you get your local changes running on Cloud Run in about the time it takes to compile your program. Jib creates efficient Java containers.

You also discovered Google Cloud Buildpacks, which are how Google builds containers from your source code when you deploy to App Engine and Cloud Functions. You can also use them to build containers for Cloud Run.

Finally, I introduced you to Cloud Build, a tool that looks like a remote `docker build` at first sight and turns out to be surprisingly versatile if you look closer.

## CHAPTER 4

Working with a Relational Database

By now, you should have a good idea of what Cloud Run is and how you can use it to run and scale your container-based applications. However, Cloud Run needs data in order to be interesting; whether that data comes from blob storage, a database, or another API, even a serverless container needs data. In this chapter, I'll show you how to use a relational database with Cloud Run.

A relational database is the most common way to store data for your application. I want to show you how to work with Cloud SQL, a managed relational database on Google Cloud. As a managed service, Cloud SQL takes a lot of operational tasks off your plate. It supports MySQL, PostgreSQL, and SQL Server, common database engines you can run anywhere. If you ever decide to migrate to another vendor, you'll have a way out.

In this chapter, I'll help you get started with Cloud SQL, show you how to deploy my to-do list demo application, and explore the various ways to connect a Cloud Run service to Cloud SQL.

Cloud Run can potentially scale up to one thousand (or more) containers very quickly. This can create performance bottlenecks in downstream systems, such as your Cloud SQL database. In the final part of this chapter, I'll explain why and show the various controls you have available to keep your database running when a traffic burst comes.

Introducing the Demo Application

The demo application for this chapter and the next is a to-do list. It has a browser-based frontend and persists the to-do items in a MySQL database. There are a lot of applications out there that feature a similar design; if you have worked with a project that had a similar architecture, you should feel right at home (Figure 4-1).

Figure 4-1. A Cloud Run service backed by a Cloud SQL database

I didn't build the frontend myself. I am using Todo-Backend (*https://oreil.ly/razTy*), a project that lets you showcase a backend technology stack. I only implemented their backend API on Cloud Run with a Go app—this allows me to use the prebuilt user interface with it.

The source code to build the demo application is on GitHub. All you have to do is clone the repository (*https://oreil.ly/36yar*) and set up the infrastructure. I will guide you step-by-step through setting up your own version of the application (Figure 4-2).

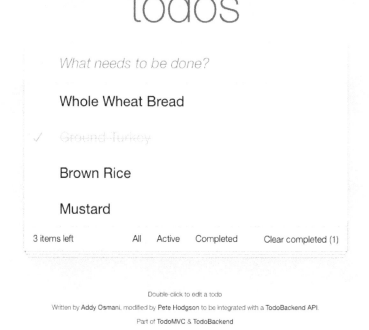

Figure 4-2. The demo application for this chapter

This is what you will do:

1. Set up the prerequisites.
2. Create a MySQL Cloud SQL instance.
3. Connect to Cloud SQL to initialize the schema.
4. Deploy the demo application to Cloud Run.

While I guide you through the various steps, I'll illustrate what happens and explain how things work under the hood.

You can run the entire app locally using Docker Compose without a dependency on Google Cloud. Chapter 6 explores Docker Compose in more depth. If you just want to try it out, you can start the app by running `docker-compose` up in the directory.

Creating the Cloud SQL Instance

The data for the to-do list will persist in MySQL, which is an open source, traditional relational database server that has been used to power web applications for over two decades. Cloud SQL also supports PostgreSQL and SQL Server—you're not limited to MySQL. As a first step, enable Cloud SQL in your Google Cloud project:

```
gcloud services enable sqladmin.googleapis.com
gcloud services enable sql-component.googleapis.com
```

The next step is to create the Cloud SQL instance. A *Cloud SQL instance* is a virtual machine that runs a database server. The *database server* can be either one of MySQL, PostgreSQL, or SQL Server, and it manages one or more databases (the actual tables and rows of data).

This `create` command can take some time (three to five minutes) to complete. Make sure to use the same region where you deploy your Cloud Run services (*us-central1* in this example). While you can run your Cloud SQL instance and Cloud Run service in different regions, it will increase query latency and costs:

```
gcloud sql instances create sql-db \
  --tier db-f1-micro \
  --database-version MYSQL_8_0 \
  --region us-central1
```

The command creates a MySQL (version 8) instance named sql-db with the smallest machine type (tier) available—db-f1-micro—using MySQL as the database server. While we wouldn't use this as a production instance, it's perfect for our sample application.

The machine type (tier) is important: the amount of CPU, RAM, and disk space you provision plays a significant role in the performance of your application. Generally, larger disks have more available input/output operations per second (IOPS); it often makes sense to provision large disks to take advantage of that. Don't worry too much about picking the right tier and disk size, though. You can resize the instance later and turn on automatic storage increase.

 Cloud SQL is not serverless: you're charged for every minute this instance is active. As of September 2020, a db-f1-micro instance costs around $9 (USD) if left running for a full month in *us-central1*. Check the pricing (*https://oreil.ly/HReOB*) for up-to-date information. As soon as you remove the instance, you won't be charged anymore (to learn how, see "Shutting Down" on page 70).

Understanding Cloud SQL Proxy

You can connect to Cloud SQL using a direct connection or through the Cloud SQL Proxy, which I think is the best way to connect. I will explain why it is better later. First, I want to explain how the Cloud SQL Proxy works (Figure 4-3).

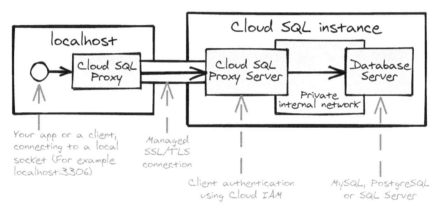

Figure 4-3. Understanding Cloud SQL Proxy

Cloud SQL Proxy (*https://oreil.ly/B2KSE*) is a program you can run on your local machine. It will automatically set up a secure SSL/TLS connection to the Cloud SQL Proxy Server, which runs on the Cloud SQL instance next to the database server.

The *Cloud SQL Proxy Server* authenticates incoming connections using Cloud IAM. I will dive deeper into Cloud IAM in Chapter 6, but here's what you need to know to understand this chapter: you use Cloud IAM to bind roles to an identity. A *role* contains a list of permissions (things you are allowed to do). An *identity* is your user account, and every Cloud Run service also has an assigned identity, a service account. *Service accounts* are non-personal (robot) identities on Google Cloud. A Compute Engine virtual machine is also associated with a service account.

One of those roles is "Cloud SQL Client." If an identity has this role, it can connect to all Cloud SQL database instances in the project. Because you created the Google Cloud project, you have the "Owner" role on the project, which includes the permissions to connect to Cloud SQL instances.

Connecting and Loading the Schema

You're now going to create the tables the application needs to run. Start with installing the Cloud SQL Proxy on your local machine using gcloud:

```
gcloud components install cloud_sql_proxy
```

Using the Cloud SQL Proxy, you can set up a connection to the MySQL database server. You'll still need the MySQL client to send SQL commands. Mac users can install the client through Homebrew (*https://brew.sh*):

```
brew install mysql-client
```

If you're on a different OS, follow the steps in the MySQL documentation (*https://oreil.ly/S1-Rf*) to install the MySQL command-line client.

Now you should be able to start the cloud_sql_proxy program and connect using the MySQL client. However, as a convenience, you can have gcloud handle this for you. (Why install the tools and not use them? Because gcloud uses them under the hood.) If you are prompted to enter a password, you can leave the prompt blank and press Enter immediately:

```
gcloud beta sql connect sql-db --user root
```

By default, a MySQL Cloud SQL instance will have a root user without a password. I'll show you to fix this soon—don't worry. You should be able to log in and get a MySQL prompt. Enter the show databases command to list all databases just to be sure everything works:

```
mysql> show databases;
+--------------------+
| Database           |
+--------------------+
| information_schema |
| mysql              |
| performance_schema |
| sys                |
+--------------------+
4 rows in set (0.13 sec)
```

Type **exit** to close the prompt and log out.

Now that you've tested the connection, you can load the database schema to initialize the tables. First, create the database, called todo:

```
gcloud sql databases create todo --instance sql-db
```

The schema is in the repository with the source code of the app. Clone the repository (*https://oreil.ly/36yar*) and open the directory. Now load the file *schema.sql* using gcloud (press Enter again at the password prompt):

```
gcloud beta sql connect sql-db --user root < schema.sql
```

You've now created the tables that the application needs to run. It's time to make some improvements to the security of the Cloud SQL instance.

Securing the Default User

By default, the MySQL instance has a super user, root, without a password, and any host (%) can connect:

```
$: gcloud sql users list --instance sql-db
NAME  HOST
root  %
```

You're protected by a firewall on the Cloud SQL instance, which stops all incoming traffic by default. However, there still is a MySQL super user without a password that is accessible to any host *behind* that firewall. I don't know about you, but this makes me feel uncomfortable. Delete the user with this command:

```
$: gcloud sql users delete root --host % --instance sql-db
root@% will be deleted. New connections can no longer be made using
this user. Existing connections are not affected.

Do you want to continue (Y/n)?

Deleting Cloud SQL user...done.
```

Now you can recreate the user on the MySQL database, and they can only log in through the Cloud SQL Proxy:

```
$: gcloud sql users create root \
   --host "cloudsqlproxy~%" \
   --instance sql-db
Creating Cloud SQL user...done.
Created user [root].
```

Using the --host flag, I restrict the user to only log in through the network called cloudsqlproxy. This takes advantage of the fact that the MySQL database server and the Cloud SQL Proxy Server share the same private internal network on the Cloud SQL instance, called cloudsqlproxy (as you saw in Figure 4-3).

What this means is that the Cloud SQL Proxy handles authentication for us. If the root user logs in on the MySQL instance, you're now certain that the login originated from an identity with the Cloud IAM role "Cloud SQL Client."

The new root user you created has super user privileges. In the example in this chapter, I'll let the demo application connect using this user; in a production system, you should apply the principle of least privilege and create a separate user without administrative permissions for your application and set a password on the root user.

I'll now dive a bit deeper into the various options for connecting to Cloud SQL from Cloud Run. When you know how that works, I'll show you how to deploy the demo application.

Connecting Cloud Run to Cloud SQL

The Cloud SQL Proxy you just used to connect and load the schema is also available on Cloud Run as a built-in and managed service (Figure 4-4). There is another way to connect to Cloud SQL: using a direct connection. I don't think you should use that, as it requires more orchestration to use securely.

If you deploy or update a Cloud Run service, you can connect it to Cloud SQL using the flag --add-cloudsql-instances. This will add a special *file* to your container in the directory */cloudsql/*.

I know this might sound confusing, but on a UNIX-based system, you can use a file instead of a port to listen for incoming connections. It's similar to opening a port (such as localhost:3306) and listening for new connections. The file is called a *UNIX Domain Socket*. I will show you how to use it when you deploy the demo application.

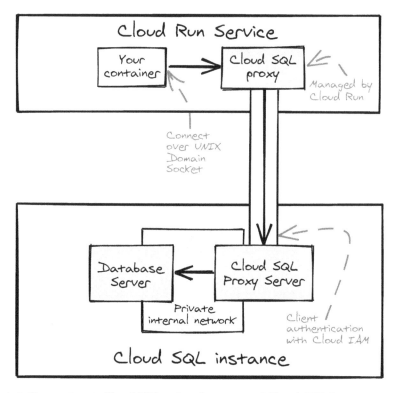

Figure 4-4. Connecting to Cloud SQL using the managed Cloud SQL Proxy

Disabling the Direct Connection

The other way to connect from Cloud Run is through a direct connection (straight to the IP of the Cloud SQL instance). While there are certainly use cases for a direct connection, I don't recommend using it from Cloud Run.[1] The direct connection is *not* encrypted by default; you can require SSL/TLS, but that means you'll need to generate client certificates and get them to your Cloud Run container securely. The direct connection will always bypass Cloud IAM, and you'll need to start managing the firewall rules of your Cloud SQL instance.

I think you'll agree with me that using the Cloud SQL Proxy is more convenient and secure than using the direct connection. To add another barrier to prevent direct connections, you can require SSL/TLS for those:

```
gcloud sql instances patch --require-ssl sql-db
```

---

1 Even when you're using a private IP, it's not recommended to use unencrypted connections.

With `require-ssl` set, as long as you don't generate client certificates, nobody can use a direct connection to log in.

Deploying the Demo Application

With the database in place and the schema loaded, you're now ready to build the container and deploy the demo application. Build the container and submit it to Artifact Registry using Cloud Build (I'm using the cloud-run-book repository we created in Chapter 3). It can take a while to build the container:

```
PROJECT=$(gcloud config get-value project)
IMAGE=us-docker.pkg.dev/$PROJECT/cloud-run-book/todo

gcloud builds submit --tag $IMAGE
```

You can now deploy the container to Cloud Run. Pay attention to REGION. Make sure it matches the region where you deployed the Cloud SQL database instance:

```
REGION=us-central1
DB_INSTANCE=$PROJECT\:$REGION\:sql-db

gcloud run deploy todo \
    --add-cloudsql-instances $DB_INSTANCE \
    --image $IMAGE \
    --region $REGION \
    --allow-unauthenticated \
    --set-env-vars DB="mysql://root@unix(/cloudsql/$DB_INSTANCE)/todo"
```

The `--add-cloudsql-instances` flag instructs Cloud Run to connect to a Cloud SQL instance, identified by its full name, which is formatted like this: (*<project>:<region>:<instance>*).

The app itself will know how to connect to CloudSQL over the UNIX Domain Socket because you are passing a connection string in the environment variable DB (`--set-env-vars DB=...`). I'll talk more about this in the next section, but first, you should check if the demo application works.

As soon as the deploy is successful, you can open the URL of your new service and fill in your to-dos. You can check if they actually show up in the database with this command:

```
$: gcloud beta sql connect sql-db --user root
Starting Cloud SQL Proxy
[..SNIP..]
mysql> SELECT * FROM todo.todos;
```

If it does show your to-do items, you've successfully created the Cloud SQL database, loaded the schema, and connected the Cloud Run service.

Connection String

The format I use for this connection string is from the Go-MySQL-Driver package (*https://oreil.ly/gEdsg*). You'll notice that it includes the path of the domain socket: `unix(/cloudsql/<project>:<region>:<instance>)`. I like to use environment variables to pass connection strings because it makes the app more portable. An example is in the `docker-compose.yml` file (I'll explain Docker Compose in more detail in Chapter 6.)

Public and Private IP

You can create a Cloud SQL instance with a public IP and a private IP. The default is to use a public IP—your instances will be accessible from the public internet and protected by the Cloud SQL Proxy server, the built-in firewall, and SSL/TLS with a client certificate (if you require SSL). If you want to improve the security posture of your Cloud SQL instance and potentially improve latency, you can choose to assign only a private IP to your Cloud SQL instance.

A *private IP* is accessible only from within your Virtual Private Cloud (VPC) network. It provides private networking for resources in your Google Cloud project, such as a Cloud SQL instance, a Memorystore instance (we'll take a look at that in Chapter 5), Compute Engine virtual machines, and containers on Google Kubernetes Engine.

Since a Cloud Run service is not part of the VPC, you'll need a VPC Connector to communicate with private IPs (Figure 4-5). A *VPC Connector* creates a network path between the containers in your Cloud Run service and private IPs in the VPC (including the Cloud SQL private IP). I know this might be a lot to take in right now. In the next chapter, you'll find a hands-on guide to working with a VPC Connector.

You can connect Cloud Run to Cloud SQL using `--add-cloudsql-instances` and the UNIX Domain Socket, protected by IAM, regardless of whether you use a private or public IP.

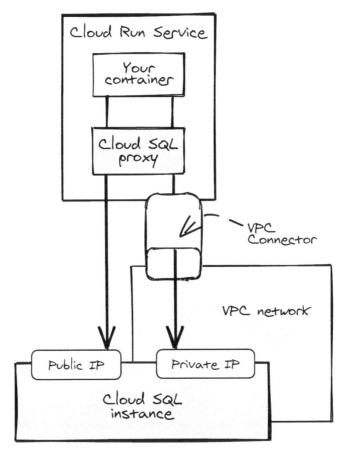

Figure 4-5. Using a VPC Connector to communicate with private IPs

Limiting Concurrency

Cloud Run, with its ability to scale up rapidly, can potentially cause issues with downstream systems that don't have the capacity to handle a lot of requests at the same time. A traditional relational database server, such as MySQL, PostgreSQL, or SQL Server, is a great example: while even a small database server can easily handle 10,000 transactions per second, it doesn't do well if the transaction concurrency goes beyond 200.

Transaction concurrency is the number of transactions (queries) that the database server is handling at the same time. When more clients are showing up to use your database at the same time, transaction concurrency goes up. To get good performance from your database server, you'll want to have low concurrency, rather than high. The optimal transaction concurrency is different for every workload, but a common heuristic is that it is a small multiple of the number of vCPUs of the machine.

Cloud Run can scale up quickly to one thousand instances (or more via quota increase) and overload your relational database. In this section, I'll explain the mechanics and show how you can manage concurrency.

Transaction Concurrency

Figure 4-6 shows how transaction concurrency and transaction rate relate to each other. *Transaction rate* is expressed as transactions completed per second (TPS). This is a simplified chart, but the general principles hold for all relational database servers you can use on Cloud SQL.

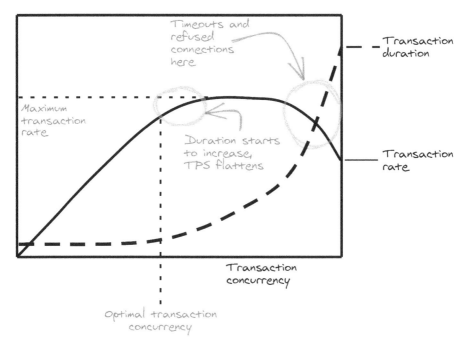

Figure 4-6. Saturating a relational database with concurrent transactions

The chart shows what happens when you start to increase transaction concurrency by adding more clients. At first, as concurrency increases, transaction rate steadily increases. However, at some point, the transaction rate curve starts to level out toward a maximum as transaction duration starts to increase. At some point, the transaction rate can even begin to decrease when transaction timeouts start to happen and new connections are refused.

It is hard to find an exact number for optimal transaction concurrency. It depends on the database (version), the shape and size of your data, and the queries your application sends. Large transactions with a lot of queries impact your database server in a different way than a lot of small and focused SELECT statements. To make matters worse, all of these factors change over time, as does your application.

Resource Contention

As you saw in Figure 4-6, when concurrency increases, transaction duration starts to climb after a certain point. The reason is resource contention. *Resource contention* happens when multiple transactions want to use a shared resource at the same time. A *shared resource* can be data (such as a row, table, or index) or system resources (such as CPU or disk). The system needs to spend additional processing time resolving resource contention, increasing the duration of transactions.

Locks are a common cause of resource contention. If a transaction needs exclusive access to a piece of data, the database engine locks the data. If another transaction needs exclusive access at the same time, it needs to wait.

Scaling Boundaries and Connection Pooling

I'll show you the various controls you can use to limit concurrency. You'll have to figure out good settings for your system by experimenting on your production system and monitoring metrics continuously.

There are two ways to limit transaction concurrency using standard settings. Take a look at Figure 4-7.

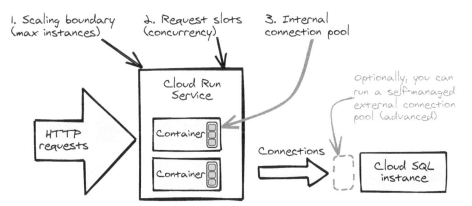

Figure 4-7. Managing transaction concurrency with scaling boundaries and connection pools

The *scaling boundary* of your Cloud Run service is the first control. It limits the maximum number of containers Cloud Run will add, which in turn limits the amount of HTTP requests that can be handled concurrently by a Cloud Run service.

This gcloud command sets the maximum number of containers to 100 for the service named todo:

```
gcloud run services update todo \
    --max-instances 100
```

If all containers are in use, requests are held in the request queue until a request slot frees up on a container. If the load increases further, you might see rejected requests with an HTTP response status 429.

From your application, you can further limit concurrency using an internal connection pool. A *connection pool* maintains long-running connections to the database server. If your application code wants to send a query, it borrows a connection from the connection pool exclusively and returns the connection when it is done. This way, you can share a connection between multiple request threads. In the demo app, I set the maximum number of open connections like this:

```
db.SetMaxOpenConns(2)
```

This setting will limit the total number of active connections to Cloud SQL to max instances × 2. A small connection pool will make sure that there will always be request threads ready to use a connection when it is freed, so in this case, "active connections" equals transaction concurrency.

External Connection Pool

You might run into a situation where you can't effectively use internal connection pools to limit concurrency. In this case, you can benefit from using an external connection pool, such as PgBouncer, on a Compute Engine virtual machine in front of your PostgreSQL Cloud SQL instance. This is an advanced setup, but I didn't want to keep the solution from you—you might need it.

An external connection pool runs on a server and accepts connections from your application. It will transparently interleave your transactions on a limited set of existing connections to the downstream database, just like an internal connection pool does.

Chris Tippett has made available a very well-documented GitHub repository (*https://oreil.ly/3Phif*) that shows you how that's done (for PostgreSQL). You'll need to understand Terraform first to make sense of the repository (see Chapter 8).

A Real-World Example

To put all of this in perspective with some real-world numbers, I want to share a real-world example. One of our clients is www.yoursurprise.eu, which manufactures and sells personalized gifts, such as custom-printed mugs, T-shirts, and photo albums and champagne glasses with custom engravings. They ship products all over Europe (their site is localized in *18* languages).

I helped them move to Google Cloud when they were leaving their on-premises data-center. The gifts business experiences strong seasonality. Around Mother's Day, a lot of heart-shaped gifts with custom photo prints leave YourSurprise's production facilities. The holiday season is another period of peak demand. In December 2019 that meant that during peak time, they completed around 10,000 MySQL transactions per second. They run MySQL on the db-n1-standard-16 tier, a Cloud SQL machine with 16 vCPUs. Their optimal transaction concurrency turns out to be around 110, which is a small multiple of the number of vCPUs of the Cloud SQL instance.

Cloud SQL in Production

Cloud SQL is a managed product, and you get production-ready features from it. The following sections explore some of the highlights.

Monitoring

Using a managed product such as Cloud SQL does not free you from all operational tasks. You'll need to monitor the instances. You can use Cloud Monitoring to set up alerts on CPU usage. If you see a sustained increase above a certain level, you might need to move to a bigger instance tier.

Automatic Storage Increase

If you turn this feature on, Cloud SQL will automatically increase storage capacity when your disk is getting full. That's one monitoring alert you can disable.

High Availability

When you enable high availability, Cloud SQL will create two instances in different zones within the same region. When the *primary* instance becomes unresponsive, the *secondary* takes over. This failover process can take some time, but it's faster than a reboot of the entire server.

For this demo application, a single zone deployment was fine (it's the default), but in a production environment, you should enable high availability.

Making Your Application Resilient Against Short Downtime

There is one important caveat: even in a high-availability setup, your application should be designed to be resilient to short downtimes of around a minute. This can happen during a failover or during maintenance. I am mentioning this because it is easy to assume that downtime will not happen in a high-availability setup.

Using a managed product like Cloud SQL does not free you from operational tasks. If you do only one thing, make sure to enable automated backups.

Shutting Down

The Cloud SQL database you created in this chapter is always on. If you forget to stop it, you will be charged.

With **gcloud sql instances list**, you can list your Cloud SQL instances that are active right now. It should list just the one you created in this chapter: sql-db. Remove the Cloud SQL instance:

```
gcloud sql instances delete sql-db
```

You also created another Cloud Run service. You can keep it around—as long as you don't send requests to it, you won't be charged.

Summary

In this chapter, you deployed a Cloud SQL instance and connected that to a Cloud Run service. You learned about the Cloud SQL Proxy: how you can use it from your local machine and that it's built in to Cloud Run.

The Cloud SQL Proxy automatically encrypts your connection and performs client authentication using Cloud IAM. It's convenient that you don't need to manage the certificates yourself.

You also learned that limiting concurrency is key to managing the performance of your downstream systems. You discovered what control mechanisms you can use in the Cloud Run service and your application to prevent your Cloud SQL instance from overloading when your service suddenly handles a traffic burst.

In the next chapter, I will show you how to deal with HTTP sessions—another important aspect of web applications. Because Cloud Run uses disposable containers, you need to store session data in a database (or, alternatively, on the client). One way to persist sessions on Google Cloud is with Memorystore, a managed Redis database. I'll show you how to connect Memorystore to your Cloud Run service using a VPC Connector.

## CHAPTER 5

Working with HTTP Sessions

User-facing web applications generally use HTTP sessions to make the experience unique for every user. If you have ever built a web application, it's likely you have worked with HTTP sessions before.

On a traditional server, you might have been storing session data with local files or in memory since this is the default for a lot of web frameworks. While this will superficially seem to work on Cloud Run, it's not very reliable. A Cloud Run container is disposable. It can disappear when it is not used, leading you to lose session data and stopping sessions mid-flight.

Examples of *session data* include the authentication status (logged in or not) and short-lived intermediate states, such as the contents of a form the user is filling in but that still has errors, or a status message the user needs to see but that can be deleted after ("flash message").

If you're not saving session data on the containers themselves, you need to persist it somewhere else. A common choice is to use Redis, a low-latency key-value store with the capacity to handle a lot of concurrent connections. I'll show you how to use Memorystore, which is a product on Google Cloud that manages Redis for you. There are alternatives to Memorystore: Firestore and Cloud SQL. I compare them at the end of the chapter.

Even if your primary use case is building stateless APIs (those that don't use HTTP sessions), this chapter is still useful for you to read because it shows how to connect to Memorystore from Cloud Run using the VPC Connector—it provides an entry point into the private network you add the connector to. This lets you connect with Memorystore and other resources with a private IP on that network, including applications you run on Google Kubernetes Engine, a Cloud SQL instance, or Compute Engine virtual machines.

How HTTP Sessions Work

I'll start with a short refresher on how HTTP sessions work so that we're starting from common ground. This will also help you understand why reliability and low latency are very important characteristics for a session store. A concrete example with Memorystore and Cloud Run is shown in Figure 5-1.

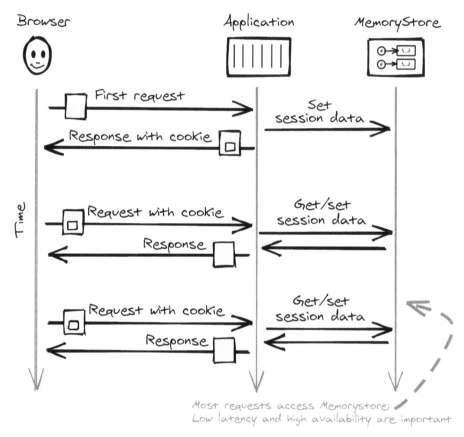

Figure 5-1. How HTTP sessions work

I'll start at the beginning. A new browser comes in and sends a first request to your Cloud Run service. To start a session, your application generates a cookie with a unique session ID and returns it to the client. It uses the session ID to create a record in Memorystore.

The browser saves the cookie and sends it along with every subsequent request, which lets your application identify the user through the unique session ID and get the session data from Memorystore.

You'll most likely need the session data before you can process any request. This makes the session store a crucial part of your application: it needs to be reliable and low latency for all requests. I'll discuss a few alternatives with different availability and latency trade-offs later in this chapter.

The cookie contains a session ID and a cryptographic signature (Figure 5-2). You don't want your user to change the session ID to a different ID and steal someone else's session, which is why it is common practice to sign the cookie.

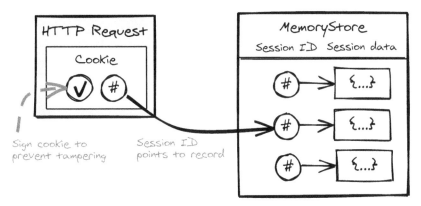

Figure 5-2. The cookie points to the session record

If you care about the security of your sessions, you should also set the attributes Secure, HttpOnly, and SameSite=Strict. The MDN documentation (*https://oreil.ly/ 7xb6v*) explains this better than I can.

Storing Sessions in Memorystore: A Hands-On Exploration

With the fundamentals out of the way, I'll now show you how to run the same to-do application you deployed in Chapter 4 and connect it to Memorystore instead of Cloud SQL to store the to-do items and session data (it supports both).

Creating a Memorystore Instance

The first step is to create a managed Redis instance on Google Cloud. Start by enabling Memorystore in your project:

```
gcloud services enable redis.googleapis.com
```

Now you can create an instance. Be aware that this operation can take over five minutes:

```
gcloud redis instances create \
  my-instance \
  --tier basic \
  --size 1 \
  --region us-central1
```

The *tier* can be a single instance (basic) or a high-availability setup (standard) with two instances. In a high-availability setup, there's a main instance and a standby replica, which is ready to take over in case the main instance fails. For our demo, a single-instance setup is more than enough.

The *size* refers to the amount of memory in gigabytes. You can increase the amount of memory later. In the case of the high-availability setup, it will not cause a disruption— the replica will be resized first.

Be aware that for production scenarios, you'll need to monitor the memory usage and configure an alert because there is no autoscaling for instance size.

A Memorystore instance has only a private IP, which is why you need a VPC Connector to reach it.

 Memorystore is not serverless: you're charged while the instance is running. As of September 2020, the instance you are about to create costs around $35 (USD) if you leave it running for a month in the *us-central1* region. Check the pricing (*https://oreil.ly/HmkWl*) for up-to-date information.

Of course, you are not going to leave it running for a month—just while you work through this chapter. You are charged per second, and as soon as you remove the instance, you're not charged anymore (to learn how, read "Shutting Down" on page 80).

What Is a VPC Connector?

On Google Cloud, the Virtual Private Cloud (VPC) network provides private networking for resources with a private IP, such as Memorystore, Cloud SQL, and Compute Engine virtual machines. A Memorystore instance runs inside your VPC network and has a private IP.

However, Cloud Run is *not* part of the VPC. You'll need to create a VPC Connector and connect your Cloud Run service to it to reach private IPs from your container.

The VPC Connector is a resource that's part of the VPC network. To create it, you choose a region and an IP range with exactly 16 private IP addresses that aren't in use.

Once the connector is in place, you can connect a Cloud Run service to it. This means TCP connections from your container to a private IP are routed through the VPC Connector (Figure 5-3). Other traffic to public IPs will still go to the internet.

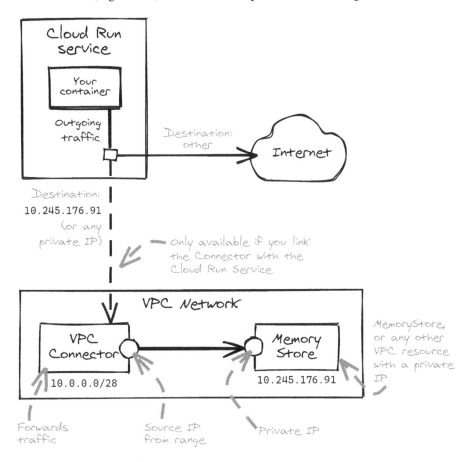

Figure 5-3. Outgoing traffic to private IPs

Figure 5-4 shows a conceptual model that helps you understand how the VPC Connector behaves. You can think of it as an instance group with virtual machines behind a TCP Load Balancer. Because they aren't exactly the same as virtual machines, I will call them *connector instances* from now on.

If a connector instance receives traffic from Cloud Run, it forwards it to the destination (a private IP in the VPC), replacing the source IP with its own IP address. The source IP is one out of the range of 16 private IP addresses that are allocated to the VPC Connector.

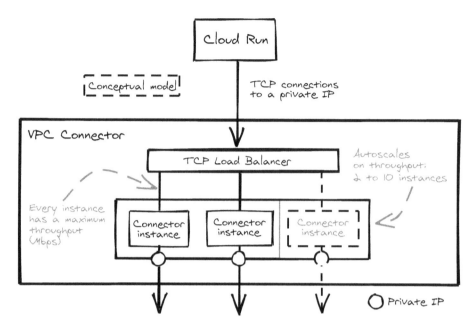

Figure 5-4. A conceptual model of how the VPC Connector scales on throughput

Every connector instance can handle a limited amount of network traffic in megabits per second (Mbps), and the VPC Connector automatically scales up when the throughput increases. The minimum number of connector instances is 2, and the maximum is 10. You can set minimum and maximum boundaries yourself when you create a connector.

 What's important to realize is that the VPC Connector is *not* pay-per-use; as with a virtual machine, you will pay for it even when it's not in use. To give an example, as of September 2020, you'll pay around $8 (USD) per month for an idling VPC Connector with two instances in the *us-central1* region.

Creating a VPC Connector

Now that you understand what a VPC Connector is and how it works, I'll show you how to create one:

```
gcloud services enable vpcaccess.googleapis.com

gcloud compute networks vpc-access connectors \
    create my-connector \
      --region us-central1 \
      --range 10.0.0.0/28
```

This command deploys a VPC Connector named my-connector in the *us-central1* region—the same region where you deployed the Memorystore instance. I'm allocating the range 10.0.0.0/28.

Deploying the Demo App

The Memorystore instance is ready to go. Traffic can reach it through the VPC Connector you deployed in the same region when you link the Cloud Run service to the connector. Let's deploy the to-do application again.

First, get the private IP of the Memorystore instance you deployed earlier:

```
gcloud redis instances list --region us-central1
```

This command should list the one instance you created earlier, named my-instance. Note the private IP—you'll find it in the column HOST, and it will look like this: 10.X.X.X.

In Chapter 3, you already built the container image. This time, you're only changing configuration, so you don't need to build it again.

Fill in the Redis private IP before you run this snippet:

```
PROJECT=$(gcloud config get-value project)
IMAGE=us-docker.pkg.dev/$PROJECT/cloud-run-book/todo
REGION=us-central1
REDIS_IP=[REDIS-IP]

gcloud run deploy todo \
  --image $IMAGE \
  --region $REGION \
  --allow-unauthenticated \
  --set-env-vars DB="redis://$REDIS_IP:6379"\
  --vpc-connector my-connector
```

If everything went well, you should now be able to visit the page on the *.run.app* domain and fill in your to-do items. If you open the same page in a private tab or in another browser, you can fill in a different list, proving that HTTP sessions work.

If you want to learn more about the implementation, I encourage you to explore the source code of the repository you've just cloned.

Alternative Session Stores

The session store needs to be low latency and reliable. Almost every request needs session data before it can perform meaningful processing.

The key-value store Redis is popular for session persistence because it is open source, reliable, and fast. There are three alternatives on Google Cloud: Cloud SQL, Memorystore, and Firestore. Here's an overview of their key characteristics:

Memorystore

> Memorystore is the managed Redis database you used in this chapter. It has low-latency key access and a service-level agreement (SLA) of 99.9%, with no more than around 44 minutes of downtime every month (downtime of less than a minute is not counted). Memorystore is not serverless, and you are billed for active instances.

Cloud SQL

> You already know Cloud SQL from the previous chapter. It's the product that manages either MySQL, PostgreSQL, or SQL Server for you. The SLA is 99.95% for the high-availability setup, which comes down to 22 minutes of downtime in a month (not counting less than a minute). Memorystore and Firestore are better at handling concurrency.

Firestore

> Finally, Firestore is the autoscaling, fully managed, and proprietary key-value store. It offers regional availability by default, and there is no operational management. There is regional or even multiregional support (in some locations). The SLA comes down to no more than 26.3 *seconds* of downtime monthly in the multiregional configuration. The latency of Memorystore is better, but the reliability of Firestore is hard to beat. Firestore also features a serverless pay-per-use pricing model.

Both Cloud SQL and Memorystore are managed products, but they still require monitoring and manual scaling interventions, unlike Firestore.

Service-level agreement is a term that comes up often in discussions of managed products. It's a document your vendor provides, and it tells you what quality of service to expect. In the case of Memorystore, it says you will get financial compensation if the downtime of your instance exceeds 44 minutes per month, while not counting downtime of less than a minute. This indicates how reliable the service is. It's not a limit—more downtime can occur—and it also doesn't say to expect that level of downtime *every month*; it can be less.

Session Affinity

Cloud Run distributes requests over available containers. *Session affinity* is a feature that sends requests from the same client to the same container (Figure 5-5) based on, for example, a cookie.

As of September 2020, Cloud Run does *not* support session affinity. I still want to discuss the feature, because Cloud Run *might* get session affinity support in the future. When it does, it will not change how you handle session data; you'll still need to persist your session data in a remote store.

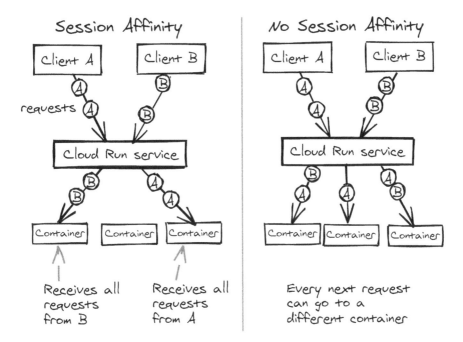

Figure 5-5. Session affinity

Here's why I think session affinity is on the horizon: Google made a proposal (*https://oreil.ly/4nNL7*) to add session affinity to the open source Knative specification (Cloud Run is Knative compatible). This gives zero guarantee that Google will actually build the feature into Cloud Run, but allow me to speculate about what it means.

Use Cases

There are use cases that benefit from session affinity. If you're caching client-specific data in memory, you'll get better performance from your cache with session affinity. Without session affinity, your cache is probably not effective.

Another example is if you're running a real-time game server and use long-running connections. If a connection breaks, you'll want users to reconnect to the same container; while you can probably rebuild the game state on a different container, that will cause a temporary stall, which impacts the user experience.

Session Affinity Is Not for Session Data

If Cloud Run implements session affinity, it will be a best-effort implementation and will *not* be useful for storing session data in the containers. Containers will always be disposable—that's not going to change. Containers can be scaled down and become unhealthy or overloaded.

Shutting Down

To shut down the Memorystore instance and make sure you're not being charged, you'll need to run the following:

```
gcloud redis instances delete my-instance --region us-central1
```

You're also charged for the VPC Connector while it is active. This shows you the VPC Connectors that are currently active in the region *us-central1*:

```
gcloud compute networks vpc-access connectors list --region=us-central1
```

Delete the connector:

```
gcloud compute networks vpc-access connectors \
    delete my-connector \
    --region=us-central1
```

Don't skip this step!

Summary

In this chapter, you learned the basics of working with HTTP sessions in Cloud Run. You gained some hands-on experience by using this with your to-do app, which persisted the session data in Memorystore. You also learned how to connect to Memorystore from Cloud Run through the VPC Connector. You can use the VPC Connector to connect with private IPs in the same VPC—you're not limited to Memorystore.

Now that you're getting the basics of building apps in Cloud Run, it's important to pay attention to security. The next chapter will explore the world of identity and access management (IAM) in Cloud Run. You'll learn how to make sure your Cloud Run service only has permission to perform operations on other cloud resources for which it has a legitimate purpose, and you'll learn how to protect a Cloud Run service from public access.

## CHAPTER 6

Service Identity and Authentication

In this chapter, I'll explore Cloud Identity and Access Management (IAM). This is the platform service that lets you control permissions in your Google Cloud project.

Especially if you are building a more serious application, you'll want to make sure that every Cloud Run service in your system only has the permissions to do exactly what it needs to do. In information security, this is also known as the *principle of least privilege*. It helps to reduce the impact of a vulnerability in one part of the system.

You'll start by learning the concepts, and to put them into practice, I'll show you how to deploy another demo application. The demo application features two Cloud Run services: a frontend and a backend. The frontend serves public traffic, and the backend can be invoked only by the frontend. To round out the example, I will also demonstrate how to run both services locally.

Cloud IAM Fundamentals

In order to do something useful with your application, you'll often need to call other Cloud APIs: you'll want to add a task to Cloud Tasks, upload a file to Cloud Storage, or connect with a Cloud SQL database. The Google Cloud APIs are protected by Cloud IAM, which verifies the identity of the caller and checks if they have permission to call the endpoint.

Roles

Permissions are granular and determine what operations can be performed on a resource. Permissions are usually tied to a specific API endpoint, such as "list all objects in a bucket." Cloud IAM organizes permissions into *roles,* which are easier to reason about.

Here are some examples of useful roles:

Storage Object Admin
> Object Admin gives you full control over the objects (files) in a Cloud Storage bucket. This is useful if your Cloud Run service needs to upload and download user files.

Cloud Tasks Enqueuer
> This role lets you add tasks to a Cloud Tasks queue (you'll learn more about Cloud Tasks in the next chapter).

Cloud SQL Client
> Cloud SQL Client lets you connect through the Cloud SQL Proxy to Cloud SQL instances.

Cloud Run Invoker
> This role can invoke a Cloud Run service.

If you want to explore all of the available Cloud IAM roles, there is one page that lists them all (*https://oreil.ly/wFndO*). It's a great reference.

Policy Binding

A *policy binding* binds a member to a role. A *member* can be a Google account, a group of Google accounts, a service account, or the special group allUsers, which represents everyone on the internet.[1] Take a look at Figure 6-1 for a visual representation of a policy binding.

A *Google account* is what you use to log in to Google Cloud. Your local gcloud program is authenticated as your Google account.

The group that represents everyone on the internet is especially useful for the role of Cloud Run invoker: if you want to make a service publicly accessible, this is the member you should bind to.

A *service account* is a non-personal identity used by a cloud resource, such as a Cloud Run service, a Compute Engine virtual machine, or a Cloud Function. In "Creating and Using a New Service Account" on page 87, I'll show you how that works on Cloud Run.

---

1 There is another special group that is a subset of allUsers, which includes anyone with a valid Google account or service account.

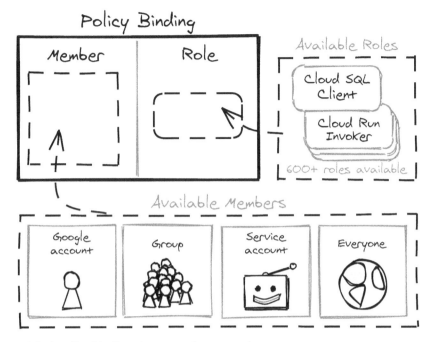

Figure 6-1. A policy binding ties a member to a role

Adding a policy binding to a project

A policy binding is useful only if you add it to a resource. Figure 6-2 shows a binding of a service account and the role Cloud SQL Client. If the binding is added to a project, the member can connect to all Cloud SQL instances in a project when added to a project.

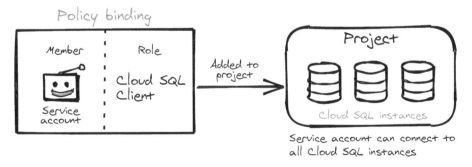

Figure 6-2. Adding a policy binding to a project

This is how you would add that policy binding:

```
gcloud projects add-iam-policy-binding [PROJECT] \
  --member serviceAccount:[SERVICE-ACCOUNT] \
  --role roles/cloudsql.client
```

Adding a policy binding to a resource

A binding with the role Cloud SQL Client can only be added to a project, and this is the case for most roles.

However, some roles offer more granular assignment to individual resources. One example is the role Cloud Run Invoker. Bindings involving this role can be added to a project *and* to a service (Figure 6-3).

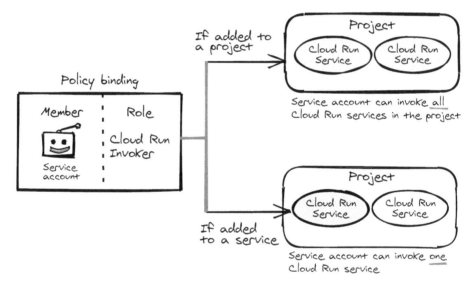

Figure 6-3. Cloud Run Invoker can be added to a project and to a service

If added to a project, the member in the policy binding can invoke all services in a project. If added to a service, the member can invoke only that service. This is how you would add a binding with the Cloud Run Invoker role to a specific service:

```
gcloud run services add-iam-policy-binding [SERVICE] \
  --member serviceAccount:[SERVICE-ACCOUNT] \
  --role=roles/run.invoker
```

If you deploy a Cloud Run service with the flag --allow-unauthenticated, you implicitly add a policy binding. You can view this policy when you call get-iam-policy on a public service:

```
$: gcloud run services get-iam-policy hello
bindings:
- members:
  - allUsers
  role: roles/run.invoker
etag: BwWvkVmZb-Y=
version: 1
```

This example shows a policy binding of the member `allUsers` (everyone on the internet) with the role Cloud Run Invoker, added to the service named `hello`.

Service Accounts

So far, I've covered how to give permissions *on* a Cloud Run service. This section will cover the permissions *of* a Cloud Run service.

A Cloud Run service *always* has a service account (the non-personal identity on Google Cloud). You can think of it as its identity. This is the identity that you use when you call one of the Cloud APIs from within your code. If you use one of the Google Cloud Client Libraries (*https://oreil.ly/LLZUe*), authentication is handled for you, transparently.

In Figure 6-4, you can see what happens under the hood when you make a call to a Cloud API from your container on Cloud Run with a Google Cloud Client Library. The client library asks the service account, through the special internal metadata server, to create an access token and sends it along with the API call. An *access token* is a cryptographic proof of identity. Cloud IAM verifies the access token and checks policy bindings before it forwards the call.

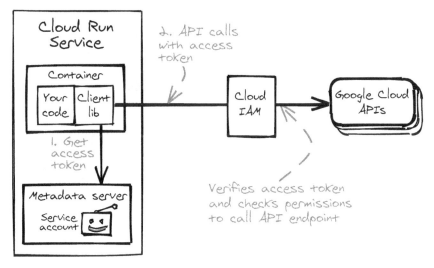

Figure 6-4. Calling Cloud APIs from a Cloud Run service

If you don't specify a service account for your Cloud Run service when you deploy it, Cloud Run automatically uses the *default* service account, which has a very powerful role.

Avoiding the default service account

To make your first experience with Google Cloud frictionless, the default service account has a very powerful role: Project Editor. This role grants a lot of permissions on *every* Cloud API. To see just how much, execute this statement, which will list all permissions of the editor role (it's a very long list):

```
$: gcloud iam roles describe roles/editor
description: Edit access to all resources.
etag: AA==
includedPermissions:
- accessapproval.requests.get
- accessapproval.requests.list
...edited: over 3000 permissions listed here...
- workflows.workflows.list
- workflows.workflows.update
name: roles/editor
stage: GA
title: Editor
```

It is not recommended to use the Project Editor role for a service account in production scenarios. Let's look at why.

A gripping demo

I want to walk you through a demo of a service that illustrates the power of the default service account. This service shows a big red button. If you press the button, the service will try to delete itself, which will succeed, because it runs using the default service account.

Don't worry, I'll show you immediately after the demo how to prevent that from happening ever again. I've already built the container image for you; check out its repository (*https://oreil.ly/lD8f_*) if you want to inspect the source code. Here's how you deploy my container image:

```
gcloud run deploy shutdown \
  --image gcr.io/cloud-run-book/shutdown \
  --allow-unauthenticated
```

Open the **.run.app* URL and click the big red button. You'll need to wait for a bit until the page refreshes. Then, you'll see a one-armed service account with a dramatic look on its face (Figure 6-5) because the entire service is gone.

When you clicked the red button, the application made an API call to the Cloud Run management API. Cloud IAM authenticated the caller as the default service account and found a project-level binding with the role Editor, which means it granted permission to delete the service.

Figure 6-5. This is what happens when you push the big red button.

Creating and Using a New Service Account

To prevent this from happening again, you'll need to create a new service account, attach it to the Cloud Run service, and carefully manage its permissions using policy bindings. This is how you create a new service account:

```
gcloud iam service-accounts create shutdown-svc \
  --display-name "Shutdown service account"
```

You can list all service accounts in your project to view the identifier of the service account that you have just created. It will look like an email address: shutdown-svc@[PROJECT].iam.gserviceaccount.com:

```
gcloud iam service-accounts list
```

You can now deploy the red button service again and run it using the new service account:

```
PROJECT=$(gcloud config get-value project)
gcloud run deploy shutdown \
  --image gcr.io/cloud-run-book/shutdown \
  --allow-unauthenticated \
  --service-account shutdown-svc@$PROJECT.iam.gserviceaccount.com
```

If you open the *.run.app* link this time, you will get an error message when you press the big red button. Our Cloud Run service is not able to delete itself anymore because it does not have the permission to do so; you didn't add any policy binding that would give the service account the permission to delete the service.

This is exactly how it should be. You can now add policy bindings, such as Cloud SQL Client, when you want to connect to Cloud SQL.

Sending Authenticated Requests to Cloud Run

The role Cloud Run Invoker lets you protect services from public access, which is useful if you want some services to receive *internal* traffic only. Figure 6-6 makes this more concrete. It shows two services: a frontend and a backend. The frontend service has a policy binding that allows public traffic. It has an assigned service-account *frontend*, which is used in the policy binding added to the backend service. The backend allows only incoming calls from the frontend service.

In this section, I'll show you how to make authenticated requests from your local machine. The next section, "Programmatically Calling Private Cloud Run Services" on page 90 covers sending authenticated requests from a Cloud Run service.

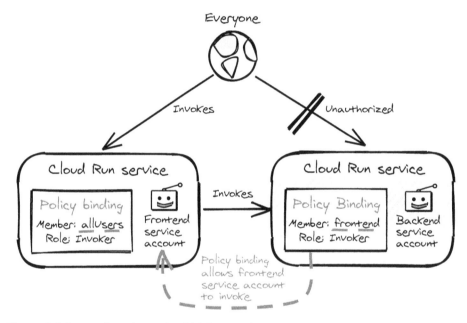

Figure 6-6. Internal services using IAM protection

Deploying a Private Service

I'll first show you how to deploy a service that allows only authenticated requests. You'll then learn how to send requests to it from your local command line, and finally, you'll learn how to send authenticated requests using Go.

This is how you deploy the inspect service from Chapter 2 again, this time with --no-allow-authenticated:

```
gcloud run deploy private-svc \
  --image gcr.io/cloud-run-book/inspect \
  --no-allow-unauthenticated
```

If you send a request to the service now using cURL, you'll get an error: "Your client does not have permission":

```
curl https://private-svc-[XXX].run.app
```

This happens because Cloud Run can't identify the request. To make sure it can, you'll need to send an ID token along with the request using an HTTP header.

Using an ID Token to Send Authenticated Requests

An *ID token* is an encoded JSON object with a cryptographic signature. The ID token holds proof of your identity and is valid for a limited time. You can get one from gcloud with this command:

```
gcloud auth print-identity-token
```

This prints what seems like a random string of characters, but there's a lot of information in there. I've made a utility program to parse and print an ID token so that you can do so safely. Install it first:

```
go get github.com/wietsevenema/oidc
```

> The ID token from `gcloud auth print-identity-token` allows access to all ID token–enabled Google services on your behalf for an hour. You should *never* share this token with anyone, nor should you paste it on a random website. This is why I've created a utility you can use to parse it locally. The package has zero dependencies, and there is just one *main.go* file (*https://oreil.ly/xo9G5*) with code you can (and definitely should) read before you execute.

You can now print the parsed and formatted token:

```
gcloud auth print-identity-token | oidc
```

In the output, you should recognize the email address of the Google account you used to log into gcloud. The fields in the tokens are specified by the OpenID Connect (OIDC) standard, and the format of the token itself is a JSON Web Token (JWT).

An ID token has a signature. It is important to realize what this means: if you manage to intercept an ID token, you can *read* the header and claims, but you cannot *change* them without invalidating the signature.

Now let's use your own ID token to make an authenticated request. Since you have the Cloud IAM role of Project Owner, you automatically have permission to invoke the private Cloud Run service:

```
ID_TOKEN=$(gcloud auth print-identity-token)

curl -H "Authorization: Bearer $ID_TOKEN" \
  https://private-svc-[XXX].run.app
```

The call should have been successful. If it wasn't, double-check the URL of the service.

When Is an ID Token Valid?

So how does Cloud Run decide if the token is valid? The request will be forwarded to the Cloud Run service when all of these criteria are matched:

- The signature is valid and signed by Google
- The *audience* field matches the service you are calling, or it is a valid client ID in the case of an ID token from gcloud[2]
- The token has not expired (tokens are valid for one hour at most)
- There is a matching policy binding that allows the service account or user to invoke the service

Note that you will not be billed for requests with invalid ID tokens since they never reach your service.

Programmatically Calling Private Cloud Run Services

To send requests from one Cloud Run service to another, you'll also need to pass the ID token in an HTTP header. In Go, there is a package called google.golang.org/api/idtoken that's helpful:

```
audience := "https://private-svc.XXX.a.run.app"
client, err := idtoken.NewClient(context, audience)
resp, err := client.Get("https://private-svc.XXX.a.run.app/hello")
```

It returns an HTTP client you can use to send requests to the service. The ID token will be attached and refreshed before it expires, so you can reuse the client for future requests. You can only use the HTTP client to send requests to the service you specified as the *audience*—the ID token is valid only for that service.

This is what happens underneath (Figure 6-7): the library fetches the ID token from the internal metadata server. The ID token contains the identity of the service account of the Cloud Run service.

---

2 Currently, only the client ID of the gcloud CLI app can access Cloud Run services with user credentials instead of service account credentials.

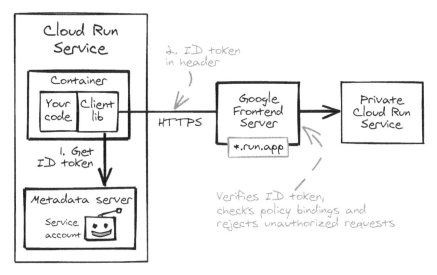

Figure 6-7. Calling a private Cloud Run service from another service

Google Frontend Server

You use the public HTTPS URL when making a request to another Cloud Run service. This means it will land on a Google Frontend (GFE) Server first.

The *Google Frontend* is a decentralized component that provides the first point of entry for *every HTTPS request* to Google Cloud. This is what it does:

- It centralizes and enforces TLS best practices, making sure your HTTPS connection is really safe.
- It protects against denial-of-service attacks (up to and including the transport layer).
- It inspects and checks authorization headers, rejecting unauthorized requests.
- It deletes reserved HTTP headers. For example, the header X-CloudTasks-QueueName is used internally, so it will be removed from incoming requests.

You should not think of the GFE as a security perimeter in the traditional sense.

Google assumes the internal network is always unsafe. When the GFE server is done processing the request, it will forward it, using Google's internal RPC framework, to your container on Cloud Run.

A Story About Inter-Service Latency

Now that you know that a request from one service to another in the same project always travels through a GFE server, you'll want to learn about the latency penalty. I did a few benchmarks and found the minimum latency penalty to be in the range of seven to nine milliseconds. This constraint should inform your design.

Let me give you an embarrassing example of how I learned this the hard way. I was working on an e-commerce product listing page. There were two remote services I had to call: one returned the product data, another the prices.

Annoyingly enough, the price service didn't support a batch call. I iterated over all products to add the prices and pushed the page to production. All was fine, until we got complaints of occasional slow page loads. I was making all the calls sequentially, and I ignored the latency every call added to the page load. I should have waited for the price service to support batch calls.

However, this is what I actually did: I naively updated the code to make all the requests to the price service in parallel. This resolved the issue of slow page loads only for a short while—my change unleashed traffic bursts to the price service on every page load, and the price service couldn't quite handle it. The moral of the story is: don't assume latency is zero, and try to aim for coarse-grained over fine-grained integration between services.

Demo Application

After a long buildup and many new concepts, let's see an integrated example with two services. I'll show you first how to run the example locally using Docker Compose, then how to deploy both services to Cloud Run using individual service accounts.

Figure 6-8 shows how the two services work together. The frontend service renders HTML (a product listing) and reaches out to the product API using REST calls to get product data. The product API service runs an embedded (file-based) SQLite database.

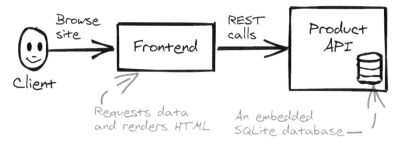

Figure 6-8. A frontend and an API service

Embedded Read-Only SQL Database

This demo shows a pattern you can use for datasets that can fit in-memory on a Cloud Run instance (in September 2020, you could have up to 4 GiB available per container, and it's likely to have increased by the time you read this). The product API works with an embedded SQLite database. SQLite is a file-based relational database. It's great for datasets that do not change often because a change requires you to push a new version of the container image to Cloud Run.

SQLite implements most of the SQL standard and makes for a great precursor to PostgreSQL on Cloud SQL, in case you want to move to an external database in the future.

Running Locally

Start by cloning the repository (*https://oreil.ly/tQhJr*) from GitHub. Open the directory in your terminal and run this command to build both services and start them (this might take some time the first time you run it):

```
docker-compose up --build
```

Docker Compose is a tool that comes with Docker Desktop. It allows you to orchestrate containers on your local machine. You use a `docker-compose.yml` file to configure a set of containers. They can be built from container images you pull from Docker Hub or local directories with a Dockerfile, which will be built by Docker Compose.

Docker Compose starts (or builds) all containers and puts them in a virtual network with local DNS so they can reach each other by name. To make the application portable, I use an environment variable to pass the URL of the backend to the frontend. This is the `docker-compose.yml` configuration file (you can find it in the repository, too):

```
version: '3'
services:
  frontend:
    build: frontend
    environment:
      - PRODUCT_API=http://product-api:8080
      - PORT=8080
    ports:
      - "8080:8080"
  product-api:
    build: product-api
    environment:
      - PORT=8080
```

This configuration file tells Docker about the two services. The `build` attribute takes a directory, which has a Dockerfile inside. I use environment variables to pass configuration (including the local URL of the product API).

Even if you just develop one service, `docker-compose` is useful. If you're interested in learning more, take a look at the repository (*https://oreil.ly/36yar*) that accompanies Chapters 4 and 5. The sample to-do application uses MySQL or Redis. There is a `docker-compose.yml` file in the repository that starts the application and both datastores.

Docker Compose forwarded the port 8080 on your local machine to port 8080 on the frontend container (it is configured using the `ports : "8080:8080"` attribute). When you open *http://localhost:8080*, you should see something similar to Figure 6-9. As you can see, I kept the frontend simple and straightforward.

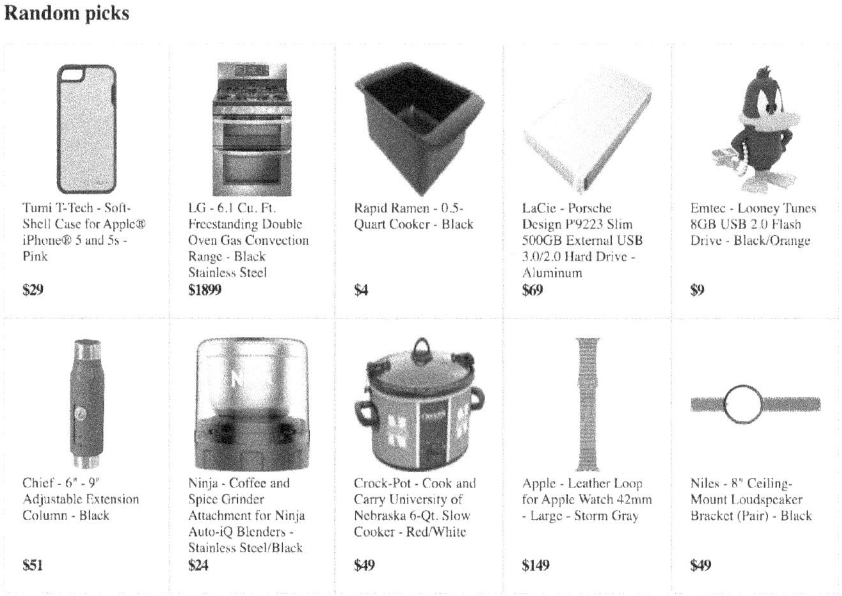

Random picks

Tumi T-Tech - Soft-Shell Case for Apple® iPhone® 5 and 5s - Pink	LG - 6.1 Cu. Ft. Freestanding Double Oven Gas Convection Range - Black Stainless Steel	Rapid Ramen - 0.5-Quart Cooker - Black	LaCie - Porsche Design P'9223 Slim 500GB External USB 3.0/2.0 Hard Drive - Aluminum	Emtec - Looney Tunes 8GB USB 2.0 Flash Drive - Black/Orange
$29	$1899	$4	$69	$9
Chief - 6" - 9" Adjustable Extension Column - Black	Ninja - Coffee and Spice Grinder Attachment for Ninja Auto-iQ Blenders - Stainless Steel/Black	Crock-Pot - Cook and Carry University of Nebraska 6-Qt. Slow Cooker - Red/White	Apple - Leather Loop for Apple Watch 42mm - Large - Storm Gray	Niles - 8" Ceiling-Mount Loudspeaker Bracket (Pair) - Black
$51	$24	$49	$149	$49

Figure 6-9. Impression of the home page

Edit, Compile, Reload

Now that you have the services running, you might want to make changes and build a new feature. Stopping and starting all services every time can slow you down. If you start the services with this command, you can selectively rebuild and restart only the changed service:

```
docker-compose up --detach --build
```

The `--detach` flag makes the containers run in the background, and the `--build` flag rebuilds them. After you make a change, run the same command again—it only rebuilds and restarts the container you changed.

When you run with `--detach`, you can't see the logs of your containers. Run this command in a separate terminal tab or window to see them as they happen:

```
docker-compose logs -f
```

While this will get you started making changes to the application, there are more advanced ways to run your application in a container during development. You can get debugging working and have faster reloads and better IDE integration. Take a look at the Visual Studio Code Remote - Containers extension (*https://oreil.ly/IojS5*) to learn more.

Deploying to Cloud Run

Now that you have the demo application running locally, I want to show you how to deploy both services to Cloud Run using individual service accounts and the principle of least privilege. I'm taking an iterative approach to get there. First, build both containers and deploy them to Cloud Run. From the root directory of the repository, run this to deploy the frontend, allowing public access. This command might take a while because it builds the container:

```
PROJECT=$(gcloud config get-value project)
FRONTEND_IMAGE=us-docker.pkg.dev/$PROJECT/cloud-run-book/frontend

gcloud builds submit frontend \
  --tag $FRONTEND_IMAGE

gcloud run deploy frontend \
  --image $FRONTEND_IMAGE \
  --allow-unauthenticated
```

If you open the *frontend.*.run.app* URL, you should see an error about the missing product API configuration. Build and deploy the product API so you can update the configuration of the frontend service. This time, don't allow unauthenticated traffic:

```
PRODUCT_IMAGE=us-docker.pkg.dev/$PROJECT/cloud-run-book/product-api

gcloud builds submit product-api \
  --tag $PRODUCT_IMAGE

gcloud run deploy product-api \
  --image $PRODUCT_IMAGE \
  --no-allow-unauthenticated
```

If you open the *product-api.*.run.app* URL, you will see "Error: Forbidden." This is exactly how it should be because calls to the product API should be restricted to the frontend only.

Update the Frontend Configuration

You now need to update the service to add the URL of the product API. Copy the *product-api.*.run.app* URL from your output and change the configuration. This time, you're only changing the configuration, so the container image doesn't need to be rebuilt:

```
gcloud run services update frontend \
  --set-env-vars PRODUCT_API=[YOUR-PRODUCT-API-URL]
```

Open the *frontend.*.run.app* URL again and you should now see a list of random products. This means the frontend was able to send authenticated calls to the product API.

However, you're not done yet. Both services run with the powerful *default service account*, and that's *not* something you should do (remember the big red button?).

Add Custom Service Accounts

I'll show you how to run both services with an individual service account. Refer back to Figure 6-6 for a visual overview. Start by creating two service accounts:

```
gcloud iam service-accounts create frontend
```

```
gcloud iam service-accounts create product-api
```

The next step is to redeploy both services and add their respective service accounts:

```
PROJECT=$(gcloud config get-value project)
```

```
gcloud run services update frontend \
  --service-account frontend@$PROJECT.iam.gserviceaccount.com
```

```
gcloud run services update product-api \
  --service-account product-api@$PROJECT.iam.gserviceaccount.com
```

Add IAM Policy Binding

If you now open the *frontend.*.run.app* URL again, it will show an error because the frontend is not authorized to invoke the product API. Add a policy binding on the product API and allow the frontend to send requests:

```
gcloud run services add-iam-policy-binding \
  product-api \
  --member serviceAccount:frontend@$PROJECT.iam.gserviceaccount.com \
  --role roles/run.invoker
```

If you refresh the frontend now, you should see products. Updating IAM policy bindings can be a bit delayed sometimes, so if you don't see immediate results, wait 20 seconds and retry.

This last successful update concludes the demo. You've successfully built and connected two Cloud Run services that run with custom service accounts, and you've discovered how to run and develop services on your local machine using Docker Compose.

Summary

As you've seen in this chapter, permissions, roles, and policy bindings are crucial to the security of your system. Working with them in Cloud IAM can be complicated, but once you understand how they work, you can ensure that every service only has the permissions it needs to perform its function—no more and no less.

You also learned just how powerful the default service account and its Project Editor role can be, and I hope that your experience pressing the big red button has impressed upon you how important it is *not* to use them in production.

Finally, you also got some hands-on experience connecting a frontend and product API in Cloud Run using policy bindings to ensure that only authorized service accounts can access it.

Now that you've mastered the fundamentals of Cloud IAM, you're well prepared to move forward and learn about task scheduling in the next chapter.

## CHAPTER 7

Task Scheduling

Most applications need to schedule tasks to be executed later, either immediately after handling an HTTP request or after a delay. In this chapter, I'll show you how to handle task scheduling on Cloud Run—because the usual approaches won't work like you expect.

On a traditional server, you handle these types of tasks by spawning a background thread or scheduling a cron job, but these approaches are not compatible with serverless environments like Cloud Run: the platform only guarantees CPU access while your container is handling requests, and the containers are disposable. This means your container might disappear, or lose CPU access *while handling* a task.

I will start with a list of example use cases and introduce you to a way to execute tasks reliably with Cloud Tasks, another Google Cloud product. These include:

- Processing an image—a user uploads a picture and you want to resize and crop the file
- Generating a PDF—for example, an invoice
- Making a screenshot of a web page using a headless browser
- Regenerating a search index after a database record updates

Cloud Tasks

Cloud Tasks is a product that helps you reliably schedule and execute HTTP requests. Take a look at Figure 7-1 to see how you would use it to handle background tasks.

You start with scheduling a *task*. You might think that Cloud Tasks performs that task, but it's not going to. *Scheduling a task* means you hand the recipe for an HTTP request to Cloud Tasks, and *executing a task* means Cloud Tasks performs the actual request for you.

This means you need to have a place to run the task, triggered by an HTTP request. You can use a separate Cloud Run service (called "your worker" in Figure 7-1). This is where the actual work happens (for example, sending the email or resizing the image).

Using a separate Cloud Run service as a worker brings two benefits: you can protect the service using IAM, and it will scale independently from your main app, making more efficient use of resources. It also allows you to allocate more CPU or memory resources to your worker; it might need them more than your web frontend.

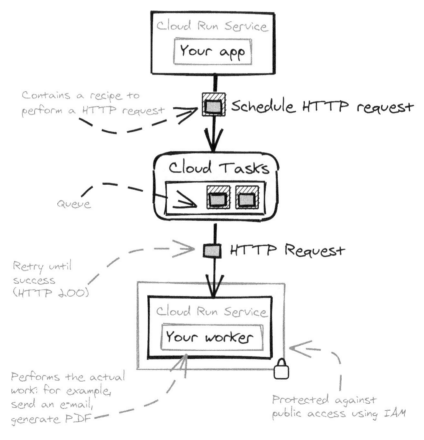

Figure 7-1. Understanding Cloud Tasks

Cloud Tasks puts incoming tasks in a *queue*, a somewhat misleading term since the tasks are not necessarily executed in the order in which they arrive.

When executing the HTTP request, Cloud Tasks retries the HTTP request until it is successful (success is defined as an HTTP 2xx status response). The retry behavior is configurable (I'll get back to that later in this chapter).

If you execute your tasks on Cloud Run, you're limited by the maximum request duration. Cloud Tasks allows 10 minutes by default, which can be increased to 30 minutes. The maximum request duration on Cloud Run is 60 minutes. The 30-minute deadline should be enough for most of the examples I listed previously. If it's not enough, see if you can split the work into pieces. If you have to process 3,000 images, you can also create 30 jobs that process 100 images each.

Hands-On Learning: A Demo Application

In this chapter, you're building the setup pictured in Figure 7-1. There are two services: one is called `task-app` and the other `worker`. The `task-app` service allows public traffic, and the worker service is protected using IAM.

The app shows a button to schedule a task on the worker. If you schedule the task, you'll need to check the logs of the worker service to learn if it received and executed the job.

Building the Container Images

Start by cloning the repository (*https://oreil.ly/D5phQ*) to your local machine. I'm assuming you still have the Artifact Registry called cloud-run-book (find out with `gcloud beta artifacts repositories list`). If you don't have it, refer back to "Artifact Registry" on page 44 in Chapter 3 and create it.

Make sure you're inside the directory and build the container images for both services using Cloud Build:

```
PROJECT=$(gcloud config get-value project)

gcloud builds submit task-app \
  -t us-docker.pkg.dev/$PROJECT/cloud-run-book/task-app

gcloud builds submit worker \
  -t us-docker.pkg.dev/$PROJECT/cloud-run-book/worker
```

With the container images in Artifact Registry, you're ready to deploy them. Let's set up the prerequisites first.

Creating a Cloud Tasks Queue

To use Cloud Tasks in your project, you should enable the Cloud Tasks API on your Google Cloud project:

```
gcloud services enable cloudtasks.googleapis.com
```

Cloud Tasks organizes tasks in *queues*. You can send tasks to a queue, you can start and stop a queue, and it has configuration; you can set rate limits and determine how retries are sent. I'll come back to that later in this chapter.

You're creating a queue named jobs. When you create it, Cloud Tasks might tell you that there is no App Engine app in the project[1] and ask if it should create one for you. If this happens, that's OK—you can create it (there's no cost to enabling App Engine). Make sure to select the same region you use to deploy your Cloud Run services:

```
$: gcloud tasks queues create jobs
Created queue [jobs].
```

With the queue in place, you can now deploy the services.

Creating Service Accounts

After reading about Cloud IAM in Chapter 6, I know you will think twice before using the default service account. Create service accounts for both services:

```
gcloud iam service-accounts create task-app
gcloud iam service-accounts create worker
```

Deploying the Worker Service

You're deploying the worker service first. This is where the real work gets done. (Actually, the app just waits a few seconds and writes a log with "Task Completed"):

```
gcloud run deploy worker \
  --image us-docker.pkg.dev/$PROJECT/cloud-run-book/worker \
  --timeout 900 \
  --cpu 2 \
  --memory 2G \
  --service-account worker@$PROJECT.iam.gserviceaccount.com \
  --no-allow-unauthenticated
```

---

1 By the time you read this, the requirement to enable App Engine to use Cloud Tasks might no longer exist, or you might already have an App Engine app enabled in your project.

I made sure to set the request timeout at the maximum of 15 minutes, and to allocate more CPU and memory. I disabled public access because only the task app should be allowed to make calls. I also added an IAM policy binding to make sure the task-app service account can invoke the worker service:

```
gcloud run services add-iam-policy-binding worker \
  --member serviceAccount:task-app@$PROJECT.iam.gserviceaccount.com \
  --role roles/run.invoker
```

Deploying the Task App Service

The task-app service is up next, and you'll want to make sure it allows public access:

```
gcloud run deploy task-app \
  --image us-docker.pkg.dev/$PROJECT/cloud-run-book/task-app \
  --service-account task-app@$PROJECT.iam.gserviceaccount.com \
  --allow-unauthenticated
```

Connecting the Task Queue

The task app also needs to know the name of the queue to send tasks to. Find out what the *full name* of the queue is by calling describe on the jobs queue:

```
$: gcloud tasks queues describe jobs
name: projects/[your-project]/locations/[your-region]/queues/jobs
rateLimits: ...
retryConfig: ...
state: RUNNING
```

Copy the name (*projects/.../queues/jobs*) and set it as an environment variable on the task app:

```
gcloud run services update task-app \
  --update-env-vars QUEUE=[QUEUE_NAME]
```

You should also make sure that the service account has permission to add tasks to the queue. The service account task-app needs to have the role Cloud Tasks Enqueuer. Cloud Tasks lets you specify policy binding on the queue level:

```
gcloud tasks queues add-iam-policy-binding [QUEUE_NAME] \
  --member serviceAccount:task-app@$PROJECT.iam.gserviceaccount.com \
  --role roles/cloudtasks.enqueuer
```

Scheduling a Task with the Cloud Tasks Client Library

To help you understand what's really going on when you schedule a task, I want to show you a code listing (Example 7-1) that adds a task to a queue using the Cloud Tasks client library.

Example 7-1. Adding a task to a queue using the Cloud Tasks client library

```go
// tasks "cloud.google.com/go/cloudtasks/apiv2"
client, err := tasks.NewClient(context.Background())
serviceAccount, err := metadata.Email("default")

// taskspb "google.golang.org/genproto/googleapis/cloud/tasks/v2"
req := &taskspb.CreateTaskRequest{
 Parent: queueName,
 Task: &taskspb.Task{
   MessageType: &taskspb.Task_HttpRequest{
     HttpRequest: &taskspb.HttpRequest{
       Url:        URL + "/" + path,       // Destination
       HttpMethod: taskspb.HttpMethod_GET, // or POST

       // Add ID Token to Request
       AuthorizationHeader: &taskspb.HttpRequest_OidcToken{
         OidcToken: &taskspb.OidcToken{
           ServiceAccountEmail: serviceAccount,
           Audience:            URL, // Scope token to URL
         },
       },

     },
   },
   // Set a 15 minute  timeout:
   DispatchDeadline: durationpb.New(15 * time.Minute),
 },
}
// Schedule task
_, err = client.CreateTask(context.Background(), req)
```

Example 7-1 shows how you send a task request. It contains a template for an HTTP request (`taskspb.HttpRequest`). There are two things I want to highlight: I'm setting a dispatch deadline (timeout) of 15 minutes, and I set an authorization header using the service account of the Cloud Run service. This instructs Cloud Tasks to create and add an ID token to the outgoing request to the worker.

Automatic ID Token

The ID token is added by Cloud Tasks when the task is *executed*, not when you *schedule* the task. That makes sense if you consider that a task can execute later due to retries or because you set the task to execute after a delay. The ID token is valid for one hour maximum.

As a built-in platform service, Cloud Tasks already has the permission to generate an OIDC token on behalf of any service account, but it requires the caller that creates the task (in this case, the `task-app` service account) to have the Service Account User role. This is how you add that role:

```
gcloud iam service-accounts add-iam-policy-binding \
  task-app@$PROJECT.iam.gserviceaccount.com \
    --member serviceAccount:task-app@$PROJECT.iam.gserviceaccount.com \
    --role roles/iam.serviceAccountUser
```

This statement binds the service account and the role Service Account User and adds that to the service account itself.

Connecting the Worker

The final hurdle is to set the URL of the worker service on the task app service. Find the URL and copy it:

```
gcloud run services list --filter metadata.name=worker
```

Update the configuration of the task-app service one last time:

```
gcloud run services update task-app \
  --update-env-vars WORKER_URL=[WORKER_URL]
```

Test the App

If you open the *task-app*.run.app* URL now and click the button, it will schedule a task on the worker. Open the web console (*https://oreil.ly/ckd4G*) and find the logs of both services. The logs of task-app will say "Task Scheduled," and the logs of the worker will say "Task Completed."

Queue Configuration

There are two parts to queue configuration: retry configuration and rate limiting. I'll explain retry configuration and then discuss rate limiting.

Cloud Tasks will retry failed HTTP requests: those requests that time out or return a status code other than 2xx. The retry behavior is configurable and can be a bit complex. How Cloud Tasks handles retries for your task is defined in the queue.

Retry Configuration

When a request fails, a retry is scheduled. Figure 7-2 illustrates a task that persistently fails and shows how the four retry configuration settings determine the intervals between each retry: minimum backoff, maximum backoff, maximum doublings, and the maximum number of attempts. I will lead you through the example.

The first interval is the minimum backoff (one second in the example). You'll then get into the *doubling phase*, where the next interval is double the previous interval at every attempt. After a number of attempts (set by maximum doubling), the *linear phase* starts. In this phase, the interval is increased every time with $2^{\max \text{ doublings}}$ + minimum backoff. In this example, the linear increase is $2^2 + 1 = 5$ seconds. The linear phase continues until the interval would exceed the maximum backoff setting. From then on, the interval stays constant at maximum backoff (15 seconds in this example). The attempts will continue until the maximum number of attempts is reached.

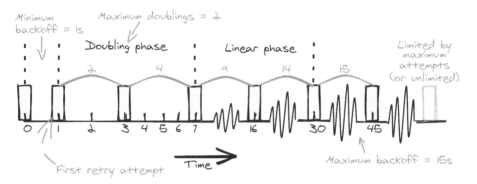

Figure 7-2. Understanding retry configuration

When the maximum number of attempts is exhausted, Cloud Tasks forgets about the task and stops retrying. If you don't want that to happen, there are two things you can do: either you set the number of retry attempts to *unlimited* (this might potentially cause the task to be retried until the end of time), or you track the completion status in a database so you can have another process decide periodically what to do with those tasks. I'll get back to this later in the chapter; there are more reasons why you might want to do that.

Rate Limiting

The rate limiting feature is especially useful if you're calling an endpoint that doesn't scale very well. There are two settings: maxDispatchesPerSeconds sets the maximum *rate*, and maxConcurrentDispatches sets the maximum number of tasks that can be executed at the same time. The default setting of 1,000 is very high. While it might work out fine for you, you should test what concurrency level is right in your case. High concurrency is not necessarily good. If you have 1,000 tasks and you run them 1,000 at a time, they might complete more slowly than if you run the same set of tasks with a concurrency of 20. For more context, refer back to the discussion about resource contention and transaction concurrency in Chapter 4.

Viewing and Updating Queue Configuration

This is how you list the configuration for the queue you've created for the demo (can you figure out when the attempts will be scheduled?):

```
$: gcloud tasks queues describe jobs
name: projects/.../queues/jobs
rateLimits:
  maxConcurrentDispatches: 1000
  maxDispatchesPerSecond: 500.0
retryConfig:
  maxAttempts: 100
  maxBackoff: 3600s
  maxDoublings: 16
  minBackoff: 0.100s
state: RUNNING
```

This shows how you can update the queue settings:

```
gcloud tasks queues update jobs --help
```

Considerations

You've discovered how you can set up Cloud Run and Cloud Tasks to run background tasks, but there is more you need to know.

Cloud Tasks Might Deliver Your Request Twice

In production, a task endpoint might be called more than once. The chance of that happening is less than 0.001%. However, if executing the same task twice has catastrophic effects, you want to prevent that. I show a possible solution in Figure 7-3.

When you create the task, your app also persists a record in a database to track the task state. This allows your worker to mark the task in progress when it starts (preventing duplicate execution).

An additional feature of this solution is that you can use it to track undeliverable tasks and avoid setting the number of task attempts to unlimited. Remember to periodically check for uncompleted tasks and handle them.

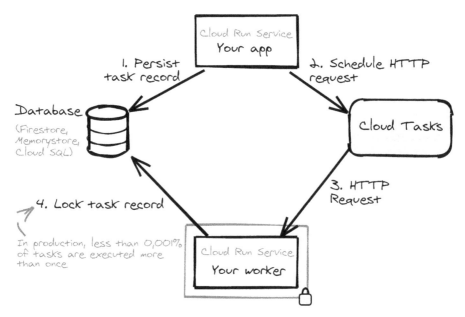

Figure 7-3. Running background tasks

Local Development

It is challenging to use Cloud Tasks in development because there is no emulator for it. The solution I use is to execute the HTTP request in a Goroutine (a background thread) in development. This is fine because there is no throttling on your local machine. Explore the source code of the app to learn more. There is a *docker-compose.yml* file that lets you run both services on your local machine.

If you think running a Goroutine is not good enough and you want to have an experience in development that is closer to what happens in production, take a look and learn if this Cloud Tasks emulator (*https://oreil.ly/Yop0D*) works for you (it's not supported by Google).

Alternatives

On Google Cloud, you can also use Pub/Sub as a queue to send HTTP requests, but it is less attuned to the use case of scheduling tasks. Cloud Workflows has been released recently and—as its name implies—offers an alternative when you need to define a workflow with multiple tasks that depend on one another chained together.

Summary

In this chapter, I showed you how to perform work that needs to be done *after* handling an HTTP request. You discovered how to call a separate, authenticated Cloud Run service through Cloud Tasks.

Cloud Tasks features automatic retries and rate limiting—it makes sure that the request is executed successfully. You learned to configure how retries work, how to queue tasks programmatically, and what precautions you need to take to avoid losing track of failed tasks.

The approaches to running tasks you were used to on a traditional server are not compatible with serverless environments like Cloud Run, so I recommend spending some time getting acclimated.

In the next chapter, you'll put to work all of the basics you've been learning as we look at how to manage your Cloud Run resources using infrastructure as code and Terraform.

## CHAPTER 8

Infrastructure as Code Using Terraform

In this chapter, I'll show you how to work with Terraform, an infrastructure as code (IaC) tool. Terraform lets you recreate your entire project using one command. If you put your infrastructure specification in source control, you can easily manage changes and collaborate with your team.

Personally, I wouldn't want to do any project without IaC. It is convenient to run `ter raform apply` and have everything set up correctly, especially when your application grows beyond "Hello World" and you add more Cloud Run services, IAM configuration, links to Memorystore through a VPC Connector, and Cloud SQL, to name a few. You can run into challenges if you are setting everything up using one-off commands or scripts.

I'll introduce IaC, help you get started with Terraform, and help you discover the Terraform workflow so you can figure out if it works for you.

What Is Infrastructure as Code?

Infrastructure is an abstract term that can have multiple interpretations, so I want to make sure our definitions are aligned. This is what I mean when I use these terms:

Infrastructure
    All cloud resources that need to be present and configured when you want to create your entire application from scratch.

Cloud resources
    Resources you can create through the Google Cloud API (using gcloud or the web console) are cloud resources. Examples are a Cloud Run service, a VPC Connector, and a Cloud SQL instance, but also a Google Cloud Project, a service account, and an IAM policy binding.

Infrastructure as code
> You use *source code* to describe your entire infrastructure and use a *management tool* to create, update, or delete those resources.

Source code
> Depending on the actual tool you use, the source code you use for infrastructure as code can be a simple configuration language, a fully fledged programming language, or something in between.

If you have never worked with IaC before, this chapter will serve as a great introduction—you are about to enter a whole new world. If you are a practitioner and have experience using IaC, you will probably still get value from the chapter. It's always good to revisit the fundamentals.

Why Infrastructure as Code?

When you work with infrastructure as code, you'll find that it is easier to reason about your system and maintain it. Everything is right there: instead of querying your production system using the command line or web console to figure out how everything fits together, you'll read code instead.

An additional benefit of using IaC is that you can put it into version control and collaborate with your team to build infrastructure in a way that was not possible before. Every infrastructural change can be reviewed using a pull request flow, just like you do with application source code. This fosters collaboration and will get new team members up to speed more quickly—and it will make changes easier and less scary.

Reproducibility is a big benefit as well. If you create a new Google Cloud project, you can have your IaC tool set everything up. Similarly, it is also easy to tear down everything you've created, which helps to avoid unexpected costs.

Terraform provides a declarative configuration language to describe cloud resources and the relations between them. Instead of listing commands to create all the resources you need one by one (imperative), you describe the desired state (declarative) and let Terraform figure out what commands to run. It will create, update, or delete cloud resources on your behalf.

I selected Terraform as the tool to show you because it is a stable and mature tool with great support for Google Cloud. It also has support for other cloud providers, which means you will learn a transferable skill. I've also found that the way Terraform models everything as a *resource* is useful when you are learning. When I am trying to understand a part of Google Cloud I don't know, I often find myself prototyping Terraform code to figure out what resources there are and how they connect.

Serverless Infrastructure

I want to dig a little deeper into what infrastructure means in a serverless project. If there are no servers to manage, why would you want to use infrastructure as code?

I showed you in Chapter 5 that when you want to store user sessions in a Redis database, you will need to provision a VPC Connector and a Memorystore instance. You also need to link the VPC Connector to your Cloud Run service, figure out the IP address of the Memorystore instance, and provide that as configuration to your Cloud Run service.

If you add a Cloud SQL database, you will need to create and configure an instance, add a database, configure a user with a password, and finally, you need to update the configuration of your Cloud Run service again to link it to the Cloud SQL instance and set up the right IAM policy bindings.

If you add additional Cloud Run services, they need to connect to one another. If you don't want every service to talk to any other service, you add additional IAM policies.

After a while, all the little things will start to add up. In a typical serverless application, you will work most often with these four types of infrastructure:

- Configuration of managed services, such as databases, messaging systems, and storage
- Cloud Run services and their configuration, like resource limits, environment variables, and linking to the container image
- Service accounts and IAM access policies
- Networking resources for interacting with services that use private networking for connectivity, like the VPC Connector

How It Works

Take a look at Figure 8-1 to see how the IaC workflow differs from other workflows to manage infrastructure. I list three different workflows to manage cloud resources: manual, automation, and infrastructure as code.

The first is *manual*: this is how I showed you how to work with Cloud Run in the previous chapters. You were making one-off changes using the gcloud command line or the web console. This is a strategy that works well for small projects that are limited in complexity.

The second is *automation*. When you are managing multiple environments that need to be similar, like staging, production, and development environments, you will find yourself adding more automation naturally to make the process of making changes more efficient. Tools like Ansible (*https://www.ansible.com*) exist to help you scale this workflow to more environments and larger systems.

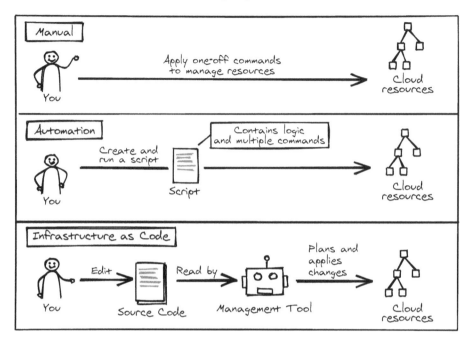

Figure 8-1. Comparing infrastructure as code with other workflows

The last workflow in the diagram is *infrastructure as code*. This is when you stop thinking about what commands to send to make changes and start thinking about *defining the desired state* of your cloud resources instead. When you want to make a change, you edit the source code and hand it over to a management tool, which will figure out how to bring your cloud resources to the desired state.

When Not to Use Infrastructure as Code

If you feel IaC is intimidating and is keeping you from getting started, go ahead and start without it. If you just want to have one service, a database, and a Redis instance, it might not be worth the effort.

However, when you're working in a team and you have tens of resources—or more—I think you should use declarative infrastructure. Keep in mind that starting with IaC on an existing project can be hard. I personally never start a project without IaC, but you will find me quickly prototyping features in a throwaway project using the web console and the gcloud CLI.

Terraform

Terraform is an open source infrastructure as code tool. HashiCorp is the company developing it and selling added value services. One reason to like Terraform is its great integration with Google Cloud, which employs an entire team to handle the integration.

Terraform uses a high-level, declarative configuration language. A declarative approach makes it easier to reason about and maintain your system, but you give up fine-grained imperative control over the details of making changes. You can't manage a gradual rollout of a new revision in Cloud Run with Terraform.

In this section, I will help you get started with Terraform. I will tell you about the configuration language you use to describe your cloud resources and show you how to deploy a Cloud Run service. Along the way, I will explain the underlying concepts as they come up.

Installing Terraform

To work with the examples in this chapter, you need to install the Terraform command line. Go to *terraform.io* (*https://www.terraform.io*) and follow the instructions to install the Terraform CLI. Make sure to install a 0.12 version or higher.

If you don't want to install the binary manually and you are a Homebrew user on macOS, enter `brew install terraform` and you are ready to go.

Terraform will need to talk to Google Cloud using your credentials. I suggest you use the Application Default Credentials (ADC). You should make sure they are properly set up. You can use `gcloud auth application-default login` to create the credentials.

Terraform's own documentation (*https://oreil.ly/L3DRp*) recommends that you create a service account and then create a key for that service account that you can download to your local machine. I strongly recommend *against* doing that on your local machine, because if you misplace the key and someone finds it, they can destroy all resources you are managing with Terraform and create new ones.

Here's an entertaining and expensive story to illustrate why I make this recommendation. An engineer on one of my teams was working on a new project. They kept the service account key file in the source directory, next to the Terraform configuration files. When they created a repository and pushed the source code to GitHub, they accidentally forgot to make the repository private. A day later, we found out that someone found the key file and used it to create very powerful (and expensive) virtual machines to use for Bitcoin mining.

There are two separate credentials managed by the gcloud CLI:

- When you execute gcloud commands, gcloud uses the credentials that are saved when you ran `gcloud auth login`.

- When you talk to Google Cloud from a client library in your software or an application like Terraform, it uses the application default credentials. Those are the credentials that were saved when you ran `gcloud auth application-default login`.

Getting Started with a Minimal Example

Now that you have installed the Terraform CLI and made sure it is authenticated to talk to Google Cloud, it's time to start writing configuration. I will show you a minimal example that deploys a "Hello World" service on Cloud Run.

When I show you how to create the Cloud Run service, I will make an intentional omission: I will forget to add an IAM access policy, causing the service to fail after the first deployment with an HTTP 403 error. I will then show you how to fix that and apply a change. This short story will allow me to explain all of these concepts:

- Setting up the Terraform Google provider
- Defining resources with the Terraform configuration language
- Creating and deploying the first resource
- Planning and applying changes (the Terraform workflow)
- Learning about the role and function of the Terraform state
- Defining dependencies between resources

The narrative of this chapter is set up so that you can follow along with the listings. However, you can also skip ahead and find the full source code for this minimal example online in a GitHub repository (*https://oreil.ly/rft_b*), which is also useful if you get stuck midway through.

The first file I want to show you is *main.tf* (Example 8-1). It tells Terraform that you want to use the Google provider with a specific *version*. It also refers to an *input variable* that holds the Project ID. I will tell you more about that, but first I want to show you how to initialize the Terraform project and explain what a provider is.

Example 8-1. main.tf tells Terraform that you want to use the Google provider with a specific version

```
provider google { ❶
 project = var.project_id
 version = "~> 3.0"
}

variable "project_id" { ❷
 type        = string
 description = "The Google Cloud Project ID to use"
}
```

❶ Reference to the Google provider

❷ A declaration of the input variable—it's a parameter to `terraform plan`

Make sure you have a shell open inside the directory where you just put the *main.tf* file. Now execute **terraform init**, which will initialize your working directory. When you are successful, the output should be similar to Example 8-2.

Example 8-2. The output of `terraform init`

```
$: terraform init

Initializing the backend...

Initializing provider plugins...
- Checking for available provider plugins...
- Downloading plugin for provider "google" (hashicorp/google) 3.24.0...

Terraform has been successfully initialized!
```

Provider

When you executed `terraform init`, you saw Terraform download the Google provider, which is a plug-in. If you look into the *.terraform* folder inside the project directory, you can see that this provider plug-in is actually a binary executable file.

> The provider is called a *plug-in*, because Terraform supports a lot of different providers. The Google provider is just one example: it is a plug-in that allows Terraform to create and manage resources on Google Cloud.

Other providers include AWS, Azure, OpenStack, and more. Basically, every service that has an API to manage resources can get a provider in Terraform. A *resource* is something you can create, read, update, and delete. People have written providers for more exotic resources, like Philips Hue lights. I am not sure of the practical value of replacing a light switch with the Terraform CLI—unless you are really serious about home automation. I think it does show a powerful property of Terraform: it is a tool to manage resources that you can create, update, and delete.

The Google provider provides the specific resources to work with Google Cloud. I encourage you to check out the provider's documentation (*https://oreil.ly/4Epqw*) when you finish this chapter.

Variables are parameters

The second block in your *main.tf* file is an input variable declaration. The name *variable* often confuses people, especially if they have a background in programming. In Terraform, think of a variable as a parameter, or input value. When you start planning and applying changes, you will need to provide those parameters. You can provide them from the command line, using environment variables or a variable definition file.

Adding the first resource declaration

It's time to add the first resource for Terraform to manage. It will be a Cloud Run service, and you will deploy a container that just returns "Hello World." You can find the source code on GitHub (*https://oreil.ly/8rOoV*). Here's what that service does: it's a container that starts an NGINX web server. The web server serves static HTML in the *html* folder. If you ever need a service that just serves static assets, this repository is a good starting point.

Create a new file next to *main.tf* and name it *service-hello.tf*. Now put the contents of Example 8-3 in the *service-hello.tf* file. This is your first resource definition: a Cloud Run service.

Example 8-3. service-hello.tf: the Terraform definition for the hello *service*

```
resource google_cloud_run_service  ❶ "hello"  ❷ {
  name     = "hello-terraform"  ❸
  location = "us-central1"  ❹

  template {
    spec {
      containers {
        image = "gcr.io/cloud-run-book/inspect"  ❺
      }
    }
  }
}
```

❶ The resource type

❷ The local name of the resource in Terraform

❸ The name of the resource on Google Cloud

❹ The region where you deploy the service

❺ The container registry URL of the container image

The snippet contains one resource block. Take some time to read the first line. In this example, `google_cloud_run_service` is the resource type, and the `"hello"` that comes after it is the Terraform "local name" of that resource. This is a label you can use to tell Terraform about dependencies between resources.

The concept of "local name" can be confusing. *Local* means the name is local to the Terraform namespace. To complicate matters, resources often have a "name" attribute as well, just like in the example in Example 8-3. The *name attribute* is used to set the actual name of the resource in your infrastructure (`"hello-terraform"` in this example), and the *local name* is used to define dependencies. I will tell you why this is important and useful in "Expressing Dependencies with References" on page 125 but first, I want to tell you a bit more about the Terraform configuration language and show you how to deploy this `hello` service.

Terraform configuration language

The listings you have seen so far are written with the Terraform configuration language, HashiCorp Configuration Language (HCL). HCL is a declarative configuration language with a limited set of "programming language" features: you can create loops, pass parameters, and create modules to capture patterns you want to reuse. I will not explain the more advanced language concepts in this chapter, but I encourage you to explore the language on your own. The basics I explain here should be enough to help you understand Terraform source code and get started with creating your own configuration.

I want to highlight one common misconception: HCL is *not* a programming language. The resource blocks are not functions. HCL is a *configuration* language. I view this as an important feature—it makes it easier to reason about the configuration.

The *resource types* are supplied by the provider—in this case, the Google provider—and are unique to each provider. This means that Terraform code is highly specific to the provider and not interchangeable between providers; changing from Google Cloud to AWS would require a full rewrite. What Terraform *does* offer is one unified workflow that lets you combine infrastructure configuration for multiple providers in one codebase.

Finally, I want to tell you about filenames. They have no meaning in Terraform. When Terraform operates, it will operate on a folder and look for all files that end in *.tf*. The names of the files have no significance. You can use files to organize the source code in any way you like.

Preparing to deploy the service: Creating a plan

By now, you should have a *main.tf* file that links to the provider and refers to the input variable project-id. The second file, *service-hello.tf,* contains a Cloud Run service that will deploy the hello service container image.

Now enter the command **terraform plan -out tfplan**. In Example 8-4, you can see what the output will look like (edited for brevity).

Example 8-4. The output of the terraform plan *command (edited for brevity)*

```
$: terraform plan -out tfplan
var.project-id
  The Google Cloud Project ID to use

  Enter a value: [YOUR PROJECT ID]

An execution plan has been generated and is shown below.

Terraform will perform the following actions:

  # google_cloud_run_service.hello will be created
  + resource "google_cloud_run_service" "hello" {
      + template {
          + spec {
              + containers {
                  + image = "gcr.io/cloud-run-book/inspect"
              }
          }
      }
  }

Plan: 1 to add, 0 to change, 0 to destroy.

This plan was saved to: tfplan

To perform exactly these actions, run the following command to apply:
    terraform apply tfplan
```

When you execute the `terraform plan` command for the first time, Terraform reads your configuration and figures out in what order to create the resources in your configuration—in other words, it will create a plan. In our example, there is only one resource. That is what Terraform tells you: `google_cloud_run_service.hello will be created`.

When you ran the command, you told it to save the plan to a file with the `-out tfplan` parameter. You should see a *tfplan* file in your directory now. This is a compressed archive. You can peek inside with the `terraform show` command. If you execute `terraform show tfplan` right now, Terraform will show you the full plan.

You can think of a plan file as a list of planned changes to get your infrastructure into the state described by the configuration.

This might all sound a bit convoluted right now—all this work to essentially execute a `gcloud run deploy` command—and the service is not even deployed yet. If you feel that way right now, let me reassure you: this workflow will start to make sense once you have a bigger project with more resources.

Saving input variables

Terraform will prompt you for the contents of the `project-id` input variable (parameter). Parameterizing the project ID like this is a good way to ensure you can replicate the entire system in a new environment. If you don't want to answer this prompt every time you run a command, you can create a *terraform.tfvars* file like this:

```
project_id="[YOUR PROJECT ID]"
```

You can also submit input variables using command-line arguments or environment variables.

Deploying the service: Apply the plan

Now that you have created the `tfplan` file, it's time to apply the plan. You can use the command `terraform apply PLANFILE` to do that. You saved the plan to the file *tfplan*, so you need to execute **terraform apply tfplan**. Your output will look like Example 8-5.

Example 8-5. Output of Terraform plan

```
$: terraform apply tfplan
google_cloud_run_service.hello: Creating...
google_cloud_run_service.hello: Still creating... [10s elapsed]
google_cloud_run_service.hello: Creation complete after 13s

Apply complete! Resources: 1 added, 0 changed, 0 destroyed.
```

The state of your infrastructure has been saved to the path below. This state is required to modify and destroy your infrastructure, so keep it safe. To inspect the complete state use the `terraform show` command.

State path: *terraform.tfstate*

Terraform will tell you, `Apply complete! Resources: 1 added`. This means it has successfully executed the plan and deployed the `hello` service. Terraform will not tell you the URL of the service. You can find that by executing `gcloud run services list`. When you open the URL of the `hello` service, you will get a "Your client does not have permission to get URL / from this server" error. Don't worry: this means you successfully deployed the service. You will need to set up an IAM access policy. I will show you how to do that in "Change with Terraform: Adding the Access Policy" on page 124, but first, I want to dive into Terraform state.

Terraform state

When you executed the `terraform apply` command, the output told you something about a state file that was saved. I emphasized that part of the output in the listing. You can inspect the state file with `terraform show`—the same command you previously used to view the contents of the plan file. When you execute the `show` command, you will see that it contains a list of the resources Terraform is currently managing along with their attributes. Those attributes can be *sensitive*. They can contain API keys, passwords for database users, and server certificates. If you are sharing the state file, make sure to keep it safe.

A great way to query the state is with the command `terraform console`. Go ahead and try it. You will get an interactive prompt. Enter **google_cloud_run_ser vice.hello.status**. You will get an array with the status of the service. Can you spot the URL?

The Terraform Workflow

When making changes to your infrastructure, you will work with the Terraform commands `plan` and `apply` most of the time, so I want to summarize how they work together. Take a look at Figure 8-2.

When you make a change to your configuration files, you run the `plan` command to create a list of planned changes. To determine what needs to be done, Terraform will compare your configuration files with the Terraform state. This is how that works:

1. Terraform knows the *desired* state of your infrastructure—a list of cloud resources with specific settings—from reading your configuration.

2. Terraform can compare the *desired* state with the *actual* (stored) state, which is also a list of cloud resources. This `terraform.tfstate` file is maintained by the `apply` command. If you run the `plan` command for the first time, Terraform will consider the state to be empty—there are no cloud resources—and will create all the resources in your configuration file.

3. In order to change the *actual* state into the *desired* state, Terraform will need to execute a sequence of create, update, and delete operations. This list of operations is the *plan*.

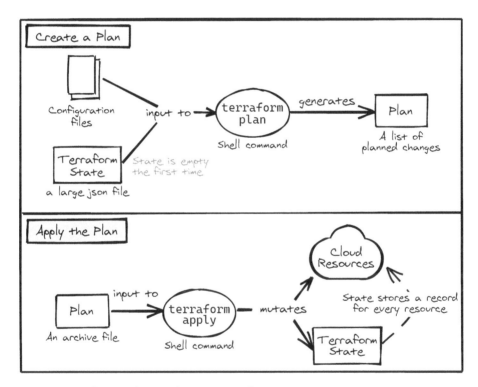

Figure 8-2. Working with Terraform `plan` and `apply`

When you have the plan, you can execute it with the `apply` command. This command will mutate your cloud resources and the Terraform state at the same time.

Always be sure to study the list of planned changes carefully. You don't want to be the one who accidentally deletes a production database[1] because you didn't pay attention to the plan before you hit `apply`. As always, when you try to make every change as small as possible and handle only one concern at a time, the review is easier.

Change with Terraform: Adding the Access Policy

To give you a concrete example of how the Terraform workflow works in practice, I want to show you how you can add an access policy to allow public traffic to the service so you can finally see "Hello World" in your browser. In Example 8-6, you can see what you need to append to the `service-hello.tf` file.

Example 8-6. Addendum to hello-service.tf, adding an access policy

```
data google_iam_policy "run_invoke_all_users" {
 binding {
   role = "roles/run.invoker"    ❶
   members = [
     "allUsers",    ❷
   ]
 }
}

resource google_cloud_run_service_iam_policy "hello_all_users" {
 service      = google_cloud_run_service.hello.name    ❸
 location     = google_cloud_run_service.hello.location
 policy_data = data.google_iam_policy.run_invoke_all_users.policy_data
}
```

❶ A role with one permission, which allows you to invoke the service

❷ A special group that means "public access"

❸ A reference to the resource we defined previously

I already covered IAM policies in Chapter 6, but here's a refresher: a policy binds a member to a role, which is a list of permissions. The policy is added to a resource. In this example, I am creating a policy that binds the member allUsers—a special group that essentially means "public access"—to the role "run.invoker." This role has one permission: `run.routes.invoke`. Using the `google_cloud_run_service_iam_policy` resource, I add the policy to the `hello` service. I am also using a *reference* here. This is important to Terraform—I will come back to that in the next section.

---

1 You can also add a `prevent_destroy` flag to prevent accidental deletion of important resources.

When you append these lines to the `hello-service.tf` file, you can generate the plan and apply it. As a shortcut, you can run `terraform apply` immediately. When you run `terraform apply` without a plan, it will first generate a plan in memory and then prompt you to confirm before it takes any action. In Example 8-7, you can see what that looks like.

Example 8-7. Adding the IAM policy

```
$: terraform apply

An execution plan has been generated and is shown below.
Resource actions are indicated with the following symbols:
  + create

Terraform will perform the following actions:

  # google_cloud_run_service_iam_policy.hello_all_users will be created
  + resource "google_cloud_run_service_iam_policy" "hello_all_users" {
...
    }

Plan: 1 to add, 0 to change, 0 to destroy.

Do you want to perform these actions?
  Terraform will perform the actions described above.
  Only 'yes' will be accepted to approve.

  Enter a value: yes

google_cloud_run_service_iam_policy.hello_all_users: Creating...
google_cloud_run_service_iam_policy.hello_all_users: Creation complete after 2s

Apply complete! Resources: 1 added, 0 changed, 0 destroyed.
```

You've now come to the point where you can finally see "Hello World" if you open the URL of the Cloud Run service. The IAM API is sometimes a bit laggy, so if you do not immediately see the 403 disappear, retry in a minute.

Expressing Dependencies with References

Before I come to the end of this section, I want to highlight *dependencies*. Most of the cloud resources you manage using Terraform have relationships with one another. In the last example, the IAM policy depends on the Cloud Run service to exist; it wouldn't make sense to create a policy on a resource that does not exist.

Another example is users on a database. There is the resource `google_sql_user`. It creates a user on a Cloud SQL database. In order to create a user, you first need to have a resource of type `google_sql_database_instance`. Just as with the policy, it does not make sense to create a user on a database instance that doesn't exist.

You need to tell Terraform about these dependencies to make sure it will respect them and not create a user before the database is ready. References are the way to tell Terraform about dependencies. In Figure 8-3, I've made this more visual. It contains another example of a dependency. In this case, it is an access control list that depends on a Cloud Storage bucket. In case you are not familiar with Cloud Storage: it is a Google Cloud Product that can be used to store binary objects (blobs), and the bucket is a way to organize them together.

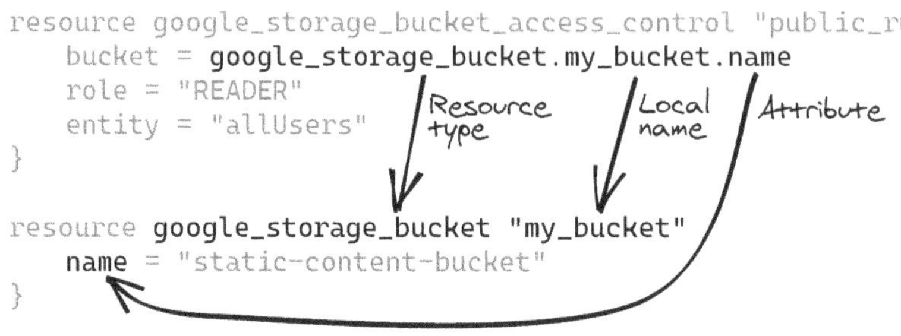

```
resource google_storage_bucket_access_control "public_rule" {
    bucket = google_storage_bucket.my_bucket.name
    role = "READER"
    entity = "allUsers"        Resource    Local      Attribute
}                              type        name

resource google_storage_bucket "my_bucket"
    name = "static-content-bucket"
}
```

Figure 8-3. A reference introduces a dependency between resources

When setting up a reference, you can use attributes that a resource exposes. You'll often find yourself referring to the name attribute of a resource, but generated attributes, like the URL of a Cloud Run service, can be very useful as well. The generated attributes are stored in Terraform state. You can use `terraform console` to figure out the correct reference to use to set up a dependency.

Supplemental Resources

I want to give you a few pointers for learning more about Terraform on Google Cloud.

The documentation from the Google Cloud Platform Provider (*https://oreil.ly/ ZRG8D*) lists the specific resources to work with Google Cloud. It is a great way to figure out the relationships between all the things you can create. I often use it to supplement the official Google Cloud documentation because the Terraform resource model makes it easier to understand how everything fits together.

If you are building more advanced infrastructure on Google Cloud, there's a valuable resource on GitHub: the Cloud Foundation Fabric (*https://oreil.ly/UaMeD*), a collection of maintained resources that package the lower-level primitives together, often in an opinionated way.

Summary

In this chapter, I've introduced infrastructure as code as a way to declaratively describe your cloud resources. It helps you to create reproducible environments easily, and Terraform configuration files are source code you can put in version control. This makes your system easier to reason about and to maintain, especially if it grows bigger.

You've learned just enough Terraform to get started. I've talked about the core concepts: Terraform state, the configuration language, and the workflow. You learned to edit configurations to make a change, evaluate the result of the change using the `plan` command, and use the `apply` command to mutate your cloud infrastructure.

Even with serverless, you can run into challenges if you are setting everything up using one-off commands or scripts.

Now that you know how to manage your infrastructure, I want to make sure that you have your logging set up properly so you can debug problems. Thus, the next chapter covers structured logging and tracing.

## CHAPTER 9

Structured Logging and Tracing

This chapter is about *structured logging*: adding metadata to the logs of your application so you have more context when you read them and can group related logs together or filter them. The *metadata* can include, for example, the log severity level and relevant business attributes.

You'll learn how your application logs go from your container to Cloud Logging, and how you can improve them with a log level (debug, info, warning, error, fatal, or panic). I'll also show you how to make them even more useful with custom attributes.

On Google Cloud, logging is handled by *Cloud Logging*. It lets you create dashboards and interactively build queries to find logs, and it shows a histogram with log activity.

In a production situation, you'll want to correlate logs with a request so you can easily view all logs that were written in the context of handling that single request. Similarly, if you handle a request and you need to call another Cloud Run service, you'll want to see the logs of the first request and the second request grouped together. I'll show you how that works by propagating a trace header to your downstream services.

Logging on Cloud Run

Cloud Run captures logs from your container and forwards them to Cloud Logging. This is what Cloud Run captures:

- Container output streams—standard out and standard error of the container process
- Every line written to files in the */var/log* directory (or subdirectories)
- Syslog—if you use the *syslog* library in your application, those logs are captured as well

Additionally, Cloud Run forwards a *request log* to Cloud Logging, which includes the request path, the response status code, and latency data.

I recommend you use container output streams for logging over writing to */var/log* files or *syslog* because output streams are a portable and standard way to do logging from a container.

Viewing Logs in the Web Console

The Cloud Run web console offers a fast and convenient way to access logs for your service. If you go to the web console (*https://oreil.ly/j5sKR*) and navigate to your service, you'll see a Logs tab.

However, the full interface of Cloud Logging offers more features. You can go directly to the logs of your service if you find the small boxed-arrow button (Figure 9-1) and click it.

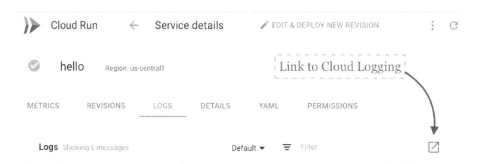

Figure 9-1. Finding the link to Cloud Logging

Viewing Logs in the Terminal

Throughout this book, I've shown most of the examples using text-based command-line interfaces, because I think they are often more useful. However, for logging, that might not necessarily be the case. If you want to find patterns in a lot of data, a visual interface is better.

Still, if you're developing a service, it is convenient if you can quickly *tail* logs (follow logs as they come in) from your terminal. As of September 2020, the Cloud Run CLI doesn't have this feature. Both App Engine and Cloud Functions do have an easy way to tail logs, and I think it's only a matter of time before Cloud Run follows suit and offers a similar feature (it might be there already by the time you read this).

Additionally, there is a terminal interface to Cloud Logging that is aimed more at machines than at humans. The next command will show you the last log from any Cloud Run service in your project:

```
$: gcloud logging read "resource.type=cloud_run_revision" --limit 1
---
insertId: 5f27e14900040088e8728110
labels:
  instanceId: 00bf4bf02d8c07f620...
logName: projects/my-project/logs/run.googleapis.com%2Fstdout
receiveTimestamp: '2020-08-03T10:04:57.429391709Z'
resource:
  labels:
    configuration_name: hello-world
    location: europe-west1
    project_id: my-project
    revision_name: hello-world-00001-yed
    service_name: hello-world
  type: cloud_run_revision
textPayload: Hello from "Hello World Logging"
timestamp: '2020-08-03T10:04:57.262280Z'
```

The output from this command is complete, and you can easily process it with a script.

Finding Invisible Logs

Sometimes, you need to do extra work to find the logs of your application and make sure they are forwarded to Cloud Logging. For example, I've seen a PHP-based application that defaulted to writing logs to files in the application directory, rendering them invisible to Cloud Run.

Another cause of invisible logs is if you run more than one process in your container and your process manager does not aggregate the log output streams. In this case, it might be more convenient to configure your application to write the relevant logs to /var/log. One thing you don't need to do is forward web server logs (such as NGINX), since Cloud Run already keeps a separate request log.

Operations Suite

Cloud Logging captures all logs of every service in your Google Cloud project, including platform logs, audit logs, and logs of your other applications. The product is part of the Operations Suite on Google Cloud. In this chapter, I will also discuss Cloud Monitoring, Error Reporting, and Cloud Trace, because they are integrated with Cloud Logging.

Cloud Monitoring tracks metrics so you can create charts and set up alerts. *Error Reporting* finds stack traces in your logs and keeps track of how often they happen. *Cloud Trace* collects latency data from requests and helps you find performance issues.

Plain-Text Logs Leave You Wanting More

The default experience when you send logs from your Cloud Run container is basic. You'll see the logs of your container, verbatim, line by line. Cloud Run does a little bit of processing before it forwards the logs; it collapses common types of multiline logs, like stack traces, into one log event. Other than that, the lines show up without modification.

Plain-text logging leaves you wanting more. One thing that's missing is a log level (debug, info, warning, error, fatal, or panic): every line shows up with the priority *default*, which makes it hard to find actual errors. Structured logging is a way to add log levels (and much more, as you'll discover soon).

Demo Application

I've prepared another demo application to accompany this chapter. It's an API that returns random items from an open dataset with Pokémon characters (fictional creatures from Japan). The abundance of data from the Pokémon dataset makes for a good structured log. You can find the repository on GitHub (*https://oreil.ly/btC5o*). I am not walking you through setting it up on your local machine because I think you'll find your way—it's very similar to every demo app in the previous chapters.

In the rest of this chapter, I'm not referring back to the demo application; it's there for you to reference if you want to look at an end-to-end implementation that covers all the topics in this chapter.

Structured Logging

Structured logging means that you add structured metadata to your logs. It is common to log in JSON. Here's a small excerpt of the demo app that logs metadata while spawning a Pokémon:

```
p, _ := pokeapi.Pokemon("1")
log.Info().
  Int("Weight", p.Weight).
  Str("Name", p.Species.Name).
  Msg("Spawning pokemon")
/* Output: {
    "severity": "INFO",
    "Weight": 69,
    "Name": "bulbasaur",
    "time": 1601626008,
    "message": "Spawning pokemon"
}*/
```

Cloud Logging automatically picks up logs in JSON and makes the extra fields available. Figure 9-2 shows a screenshot of Cloud Logging with structured logs. I clicked on a log event to expand and added the name and weight of the Pokémon to the *summary line* of the log. You can see them in the green pills that lead the line.

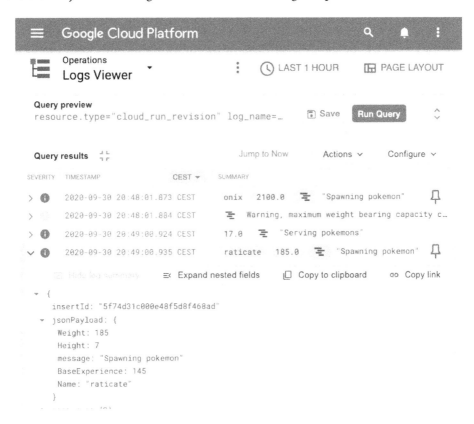

Figure 9-2. Structured log attributes in the summary line

You can also search logs using custom attributes. For example, you can view all logs that relate to the same Pokémon, or only logs that handle extremely heavy Pokémon.

Client Libraries

Instead of logging JSON-formatted messages, you can also send logs directly to the Cloud Logging API using the Cloud Logging client libraries (*https://oreil.ly/EP78E*). This is how they work: you write logs using the library, which buffers the logs in memory and sends them to the Cloud Logging API periodically.

The Cloud Logging client libraries bypass the container output streams and connect directly to the Google Cloud Logging API. This hurts the portability of your app, reducing your ability to deploy it elsewhere (out of Google Cloud or on your local machine).

Cloud Logging is already integrated into Cloud Run; the only thing you need to do is write logs in the proper format. This is why I'll show you how to write structured JSON logs from your container.

Structured Logging in Other Languages

I'm showing the examples using the zerolog package in Go, but you can still benefit if you use a different programming language. *Zerolog* is a Go package that writes JSON-formatted logs using zero memory allocation, which makes it very performant. Other languages have similar libraries; structured logging has been around for a while.

The only thing you need to make sure of is that the structure of your JSON messages matches what Cloud Logging expects. If you're searching for a plug-in, keep in mind that the Cloud Logging product was previously called Stackdriver. The structure of the messages is not complex, so you can also roll your own plug-in (*https://oreil.ly/zTF62*).

How to Use Log Levels

If you're careful and disciplined about when to use which log level, you'll get more value out of your logs. In Table 9-1 , you can find a list of log levels and guidance for when to use them. The first column lists the zerolog function you use. Note that these are different from the Cloud Logging levels.

Table 9-1. Log severity levels and when to use them

Cloud Logging level	Zerolog function	When to use
DEBUG	Debug()	Debug logs are very verbose, meant for local debugging only, and are usually disabled on production.
INFO	Info()	Regular status messages: "Updated record."
WARNING	Warn()	Warnings might be errors: "Record not found," "Configuration not found, using default."
ERROR	Error()	An exception happened. "Failed to save record." You should aim for zero errors in your logs: don't log errors as part of the normal flow.
CRITICAL	Fatal()	A critical error needs to be corrected. For example, the database is not available even after retries. Calling Fatal() stops the container, and your user will get a "Service Unavailable - HTTP 503" response.
ALERT	Panic()	You should use Panic() if your application is seriously broken and someone should be alerted to take action immediately. Zerolog will also call the built-in panic function, stopping the execution of your program with a stack trace.

Capturing Panics

If you log an event using `zerolog.Panic()`, it logs the message and calls Go's built-in function, `panic`. A panic can also occur when your program encounters an index out of range or a nil pointer. A panicking program prints a plain-text stack trace and quits.

Even though the stack trace prints in plain text, Cloud Logging detects and adds a log event with the *default* log level (unspecified), and Cloud Error Reporting (*https://oreil.ly/_EmPS*) notices and starts to track the event (Figure 9-3). You don't need to configure anything for this to work, and Cloud Error Reporting detects stack traces from other languages, too.

Sensitive Information and Logging

I want to make you aware of the security implications of adding more metadata to your logs. I recommend keeping personally identifiable or otherwise sensitive information out of the logs. I suggest you do a search online for "plain text password in logs" to get an idea of what can happen if you do put sensitive information in your logs (this issue is not limited to structured logs).

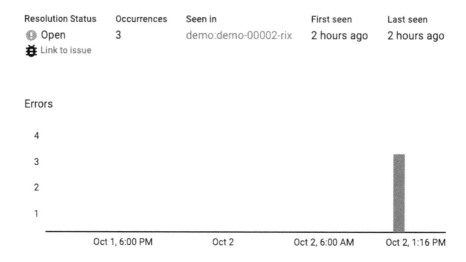

2020/10/02 08:51:52 http: panic serving: Panic

net/http.(*conn).serve.**func1** (server.go:1801)

Resolution Status	Occurrences	Seen in	First seen	Last seen
🔵 Open	3	demo:demo-00002-rix	2 hours ago	2 hours ago
🐞 Link to issue				

Errors

```
4

3

2

1
           Oct 1, 6:00 PM        Oct 2        Oct 2, 6:00 AM        Oct 2, 1:16 PM
```

Stack trace sample

Parsed   Raw

```
2020/10/02 08: 51:52 http: panic serving: Panic
    at net/http.(*conn).serve.func1 (server.go:1801)
    at panic (/usr/local/go/src/runtime/panic.go:975)
    at github.com/rs/zerolog.(*Logger).Panic.func1 (log.go:345)
    at github.com/rs/zerolog.(*Event).msg (event.go:147)
    at github.com/rs/zerolog.(*Event).Msg (event.go:106)
    at main.PanicHandler (main.go:62)
    at net/http.HandlerFunc.ServeHTTP (server.go:2042)
    at github.com/gorilla/mux.(*Router).ServeHTTP (mux.go:210)
    at github.com/yfuruyama/crzerolog.(*middleware).ServeHTTP (http.go:39)
    at go.opencensus.io/plugin/ochttp.(*Handler).ServeHTTP (server.go:92)
    at net/http.serverHandler.ServeHTTP (server.go:2843)
    at net/http.(*conn).serve (server.go:1925)
```

Figure 9-3. Cloud Error Reporting finds panics

Local Development

I don't know about you, but reading JSON-formatted log messages in a terminal during development is not something I'm excited about. It's a good thing you don't have to: the zerolog package has `zerolog.ConsoleWriter`, which outputs readable (and colorized) logs for use in development.

Request Context

In production scenarios, it is useful if you can click on a log event and view all other logs that were written while handling the same request. If your service is handling a lot of requests at the same time, this is an indispensable feature: your application can generate many log messages while handling a single request. If many requests happen at the same time, all the messages become interleaved, and it becomes difficult to identify which logs belong together.

The Google Frontend (GFE) adds a trace header (`X-Cloud-Trace-Context`) to all incoming requests (Figure 9-4). A *trace header* contains a unique trace ID. If you take the trace ID and add it to all logs related to handling the request, they will show up together in Cloud Logging.

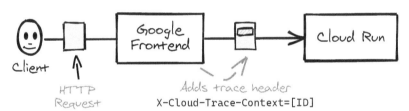

Figure 9-4. The Google Frontend adds a trace header to requests

Example 9-1 offers an example of how you can add the trace ID to the logs using the `crzerolog` package (*https://oreil.ly/sopab*) by Yuki Furuyama.

Example 9-1. Adding the trace ID to the logs

```
func main() {
    rootLogger := zerolog.New(os.Stdout)
    // Create an HTTP handler that adds request context to logs
    loggingHandler := crzerolog.InjectLogger(&rootLogger)

    mux := http.NewServeMux()
    mux.HandleFunc("/", func(w http.ResponseWriter, r *http.Request) {
        // Retrieve the logger from the request
        logger := log.Ctx(r.Context())

        logger.Debug().Msg("1st")
```

```
        logger.Info().Msg("2nd")
        logger.Error().Msg("3rd")
    })

    // Wrap the logging handler around the http handler
    handler := loggingHandler(mux)

    if err := http.ListenAndServe(":8080", handler); err != nil {
        log.Fatal().Msg("Can't start service")
    }
}
```

The package lets you pull a logger from the request context. If you use that logger, the trace ID is automatically added to the logs, using the attribute names that Cloud Logging expects. Here's an example:

```
{
  "severity": "DEBUG",
  "logging.googleapis.com/trace": "[trace ID]",

  "time": "2020-10-02...",
  "message": "1st"
}
```

The `logging.googleapis.com/trace` attribute holds the trace ID, which Cloud Logging uses to link logs to a request.

To give you an impression of how useful request context is, I've deployed the code from Example 9-1 to Cloud Run and sent 1,000 requests to the service at the same time. Figure 9-5 shows an excerpt from the results: there are nine log events from three different requests, logged in the *exact same* millisecond. If not for the request context, it would have been hard to make sense of these logs. In the screenshot, I've expanded one request (in the box with the arrow) to see all logs that were written while handling only that request. I don't know about you, but I think this clearly shows the usefulness of having a request context.

If you use the `crzerolog` package, it also adds the source location to logs: it tells you the message "1st" was logged on line 21 of *main.go*. (Click "Expand nested fields" to see all attributes.)

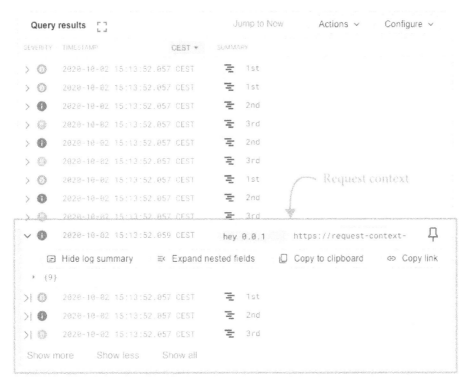

Figure 9-5. Making sense of 1,000 concurrent requests

Trace Context

If you handle a request and you need to call another Cloud Run service, you'll want to see the logs of the first request and the second request grouped together. Especially if your app is divided into multiple (micro)services working together, this is a feature you won't want to live without; if you have a problem in one of the downstream services, you want to be aware of what happened in the service that called it.

Distributed tracing is a mature and complex topic, and I can only scratch the surface of the topic here (I'm taking a very pragmatic approach). For a comprehensive view, I recommend *Distributed Tracing in Practice* by Austin Parker, Daniel Spoonhower, Jonathan Mace, Ben Sigelman, and Rebecca Isaacs (O'Reilly, 2020).

Forwarding Trace ID

If you capture the incoming trace header and forward the trace ID to requests *from* your service, Cloud Logging adds all requests to the same trace. Figure 9-6, shows what happens when you send a request to a Cloud Run service, which in turn sends a request to a second Cloud Run service. The GFE always adds an X-Cloud-Trace-Context header to incoming requests and preserves the trace ID on incoming requests that already have an X-Cloud-Trace-Context header.

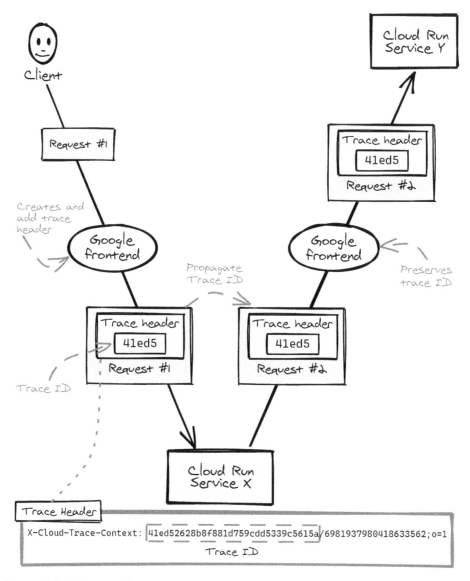

Figure 9-6. Understanding trace context propagation

Now that you understand how it works, let's see how you can implement trace ID forwarding in Go. In Chapter 6, I showed you how to send authenticated requests to other services using the idtoken package. The idtoken package also supports trace context propagation; however, getting it right requires some orchestration. Here are the key steps:

1. Write your logs using the `crzerolog` package to add the trace ID to the logs (covered in the last example).

2. Add the trace ID to all incoming requests in a way that the `idtoken` package understands (using Go's request context).

3. Pass that request context from an incoming request to the outgoing request and make requests using the `idtoken` HTTP client.

You can also use the `idtoken` package to send requests to public Cloud Run services—an ID token only identifies your request.

Preparing All Incoming Requests with the Trace ID

The `idtoken` package needs the trace ID on the request context to be compatible with the open source distributed-tracing tool OpenCensus. You can wrap your HTTP handler with an OpenCensus one:

```
// "go.opencensus.io/plugin/ochttp"
// "contrib.go.opencensus.io/exporter/stackdriver/propagation"
httpHandler := &ochttp.Handler{
  Propagation: &propagation.HTTPFormat{},
  Handler:     handler,
}
http.ListenAndServe(":8080", httpHandler)
```

Now that the trace ID is in the request context of all *incoming* requests, you'll need to pass it to the idtoken client when you make *outgoing* requests.

Passing Request Context to Outgoing Requests

When you make a request using the `idtoken` package, you should pass the request context of the incoming request to the outgoing request (`WithContext`):

```
URL := "https://[SERVICE].run.app"
client, _ := idtoken.NewClient(context.Background(), URL)


mux.HandleFunc("/", func(w http.ResponseWriter, r *http.Request) {
  req, _ := http.NewRequest("GET", URL, nil)
  req = req.WithContext(r.Context()) // Pass context
  client.Do(req)
})
```

Example 9-2 shows an end-to-end example you can deploy to Cloud Run. It features a service with two endpoints. The first endpoint is "/". If you request it, it logs the message "1st" and uses the idtoken package to make a second request to the endpoint "/call" on the same service using the external *.run.app* URL of the service. The "/call" endpoint logs the message "2nd".

Example 9-2. Final listing of the end-to-end demo

```go
package main

import (
    "context"
    "os"

    "contrib.go.opencensus.io/exporter/stackdriver/propagation"
    "github.com/rs/zerolog"
    "github.com/rs/zerolog/log"
    "github.com/yfuruyama/crzerolog"
    "go.opencensus.io/plugin/ochttp"
    "google.golang.org/api/idtoken"

    "net/http"
)

func main() {

    mux := http.NewServeMux()
    mux.HandleFunc("/", func(w http.ResponseWriter, r *http.Request) {
        client, _ := idtoken.NewClient(context.Background(), r.Host)
        log.Ctx(r.Context()).Info().Msg("1st")
        req, _ := http.NewRequest("GET", "https://"+r.Host+"/call", nil)
        req = req.WithContext(r.Context())
        client.Do(req)
    })
    mux.HandleFunc("/call",
      func(w http.ResponseWriter, r *http.Request) {
        log.Ctx(r.Context()).Info().Msg("2nd")
    })

    rootLogger := zerolog.New(os.Stdout)
    middleware := crzerolog.InjectLogger(&rootLogger)
    handler := middleware(mux)

    httpHandler := &ochttp.Handler{
        Propagation: &propagation.HTTPFormat{},
        Handler:     handler,
    }
    if err := http.ListenAndServe(":8080", httpHandler); err != nil {
        log.Fatal().Msg("Can't start service")
    }
}
```

Viewing Trace Context in Cloud Logging

You can deploy Example 9-2 as a Cloud Run service. It makes a request to itself and forwards the trace ID. This is how you can view the trace in Cloud Logging (Figure 9-7). Take any log, click on the pill with the blue bars, and "Show all logs for this trace." In the figure, you can see two HTTP requests—one from my Chrome browser and one from the Go HTTP client—and the two logs, which were written by different requests.

Figure 9-7. Showing all logs for one trace across different request contexts

Additional Resources About Tracing

I've deliberately taken a pragmatic approach to explaining distributed tracing, and you should know that I've only scratched the surface of what is possible. You can create custom spans (not just requests), control the sampling rate, and increase visibility into your entire stack. This is where Cloud Trace comes in. Refer to the documentation (*https://oreil.ly/Nre2f*) to learn how to configure Cloud Trace in a Go app (you'll use the same OpenCensus library).

Log-Based Metrics with Cloud Monitoring

Cloud Monitoring (*https://oreil.ly/0cYjy*) lets you monitor Cloud Run system metrics like container CPU and memory (utilization and allocation), as well as request latency and count.

Structured logging brings a lot of useful additional data to your logs in Cloud Logging, and Cloud Monitoring can ingest the data. This means you can create charts and set up alerts with log-based metrics. Figure 9-8 shows a chart that tracks the weight of the Pokémon I'm spawning (take a look at the demo app).

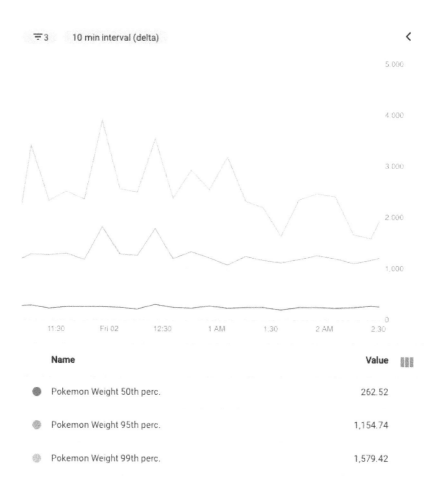

Name	Value	▮▮▮
● Pokemon Weight 50th perc.	262.52	
◉ Pokemon Weight 95th perc.	1,154.74	
◉ Pokemon Weight 99th perc.	1,579.42	

Figure 9-8. Charting Pokémon weight

To create a log-based metric, go to the "Logs-based metrics" tab in Cloud Logging and click the "Create Metric" button.

Summary

Logging is an important part of building production-ready applications. In this chapter, I've shown you how to improve your logging by adding metadata attributes; this is known as structured logging. To summarize, here's what you get when you use structured logging on Cloud Run:

Log level

The log level represents the importance of a log event (debug, info, warning, error, fatal, panic). This is the most common type of metadata, and you can't really live without it.

Business metadata

If you can link logs to logical concepts like an order or a product, that can help you make sense of them and find patterns. However, be careful not to add personal information.

Source code location

If you know which exact line of code printed a log, you won't have to search through your codebase trying to figure out where it came from.

Request context

If an error happens, it is useful to read all the logs that were written while handling that request.

Trace context

If you propagate the request context when you make calls to downstream Cloud Run services, you can see the logs of all those requests together.

I like that Cloud Run integrates with Cloud Logging without forcing you to use vendor-specific libraries and tooling, and instead lets you use open source libraries to improve your logging experience.

When you step back from the day-to-day concerns of running your system and think about a future—one that might not include Google Cloud—it's good to look at alternatives. In Chapter 10, I'll show hands-on what it means that Cloud Run is compatible with the Knative specification.

Cloud Run and Knative Serving

Cloud Run is API compatible with the open source project Knative Serving. That means that you are able to take a service from Cloud Run to Knative Serving without much (or with zero) effort.

In this chapter, I'll show you how. I'll walk you through installing Knative Serving on your local machine and show you how to deploy a container to both Cloud Run and your local Knative Serving using the exact same service definition.

Knative Serving is installed on top of Kubernetes, the open source container orchestrator. I'll explain the architecture of Kubernetes so you can build a mental model of how it works and understand how Knative Service works under the hood.

As an independent open source project, Knative Serving might start to include features that are not available on Cloud Run. However, I think it's likely that Cloud Run will always support a subset of features of Knative Serving, if not all of them.

Portability

I don't think you should run Knative Serving on your local machine as a development environment. Docker offers a lightweight approach to orchestrating containers on your local machine with Docker Compose, as you discovered in Chapter 6.

You might wonder, then: why should I go through the trouble of this demonstration? This is why: building an application on a vendor-controlled platform carries a certain risk. Your vendor might change pricing or other terms unilaterally, making the platform less attractive for you. *Portability* refers to how easy it is to move your application to a different product or vendor, and I think it is important.

Another scenario that might drive you toward Knative Serving is when regulations require you to run your software and store your data in a geographic location where Google Cloud has no presence (such as the Chinese mainland).

This chapter will help you build a more concrete and real view of what your options are if you want to move your application off Google Cloud someday. That day might never come, but I think it is good to be prepared.

What Is Knative Serving?

The primary goal of Knative Serving is to provide developers with a good abstraction for operating a stateless service that is container based and request driven and that scales from zero to many containers automatically.

Knative Serving has the same resource model as Cloud Run. What this means is that the primary resources you interact with as a developer are the same. Just like on Cloud Run, you'll create a service to deploy your container, and Knative creates a new immutable revision every time you change the service. A *revision* is a combination of your container image—at that point in time—and runtime configurations, such as environment variables and resource requirements (CPU and memory).

The runtime behavior of Knative is also the same. The individual containers are disposable, and your service automatically scales from zero containers to many, closely tracking demand.

Cloud Run Is Not Managed Knative Serving

A common misconception is that Cloud Run is a managed version of Knative Serving. This is not the case. Cloud Run is a *compatible* but completely separate and proprietary implementation of the same specification. Cloud Run runs directly on top of Borg, the hyper-scalable container infrastructure that Google uses to power Google Search, Maps, Gmail, and App Engine.

Knative Serving on Google Cloud

If you want to use Knative Serving, you can run a completely self-managed solution on your own infrastructure, or Cloud Run, and everything in between, as I show in Figure 10-1.

Knative provides an abstraction layer that allows you, as a developer, to have a serverless developer experience, regardless of whether you manage your own infrastructure.

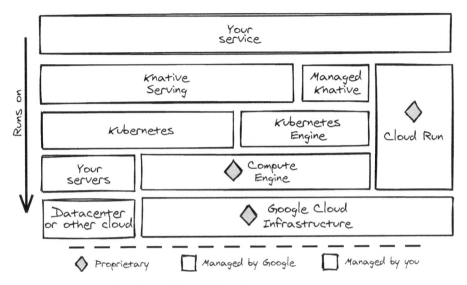

Figure 10-1. Knative Serving on Google Cloud

Understanding Kubernetes

Since Knative Serving is an extension you can add to a Kubernetes cluster, I'll introduce you to Kubernetes. If you're already familiar with Kubernetes, this part will be a good review of the fundamentals. I'll give you the 30,000-foot view and provide you with references to additional resources along the way.

Coming out of this section, you should understand how you interact with Kubernetes and have a high-level understanding of the architecture of Kubernetes. This will help you understand Knative Serving.

A *Kubernetes cluster* is a set of nodes (servers) that run containers. While it is common to use a managed Kubernetes cluster from one of the vendors, you can also run Kubernetes on physical hardware in your own datacenter and manage it yourself.

In its essence, Kubernetes is a container orchestrator. If you start a container, Kubernetes figures out on which node to start it and makes sure network traffic can get to the container.

The architecture of Kubernetes supports large deployments. Google reports real-world deployments running up to 15,000 nodes (*https://oreil.ly/3XE9o*) using Google Kubernetes Engine (GKE) clusters. GKE is Google's managed Kubernetes offering.

Figure 10-2 shows an overview of the components that make up Kubernetes.

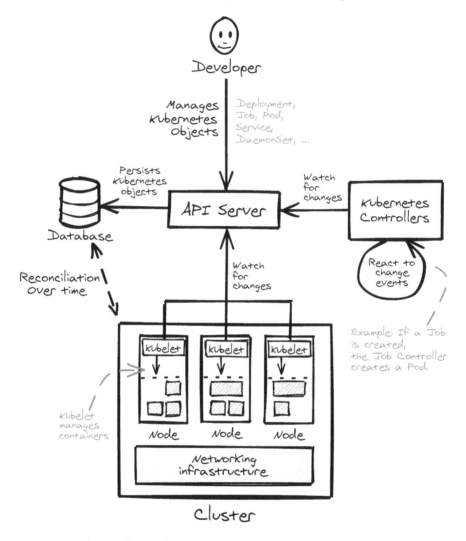

Figure 10-2. Understanding Kubernetes

API Server

The API server sits at the center of Kubernetes. You interact with it using a client, like the command-line client kubectl. For example, if you want to start a single container with the web server NGINX, you run this command to send a request to the API server:

```
kubectl create deployment --image=docker.io/library/nginx nginx
```

The Kubernetes API is *resource based*: you create, read, update, or delete Kubernetes resources.

Kubernetes Resources

A deployment is one of the core Kubernetes resources you can use to model your application. A *deployment* represents a set of containers. If a container fails or becomes unhealthy, Kubernetes restarts it. The containers in the deployment are specified using a Pod resource—another core Kubernetes resource. *Pods* are the simplest Kubernetes resources, and they represent one container (or several working together) in your cluster.

 If you want to learn more about how to build and deliver applications on Kubernetes, I recommend the book *Kubernetes: Up and Running*, 2nd Edition, by Brendan Burns, Joe Beda, and Kelsey Hightower (O'Reilly, 2019). The book features several chapters dedicated to understanding key Kubernetes resources, including Deployments, Pods, DaemonSets, and Jobs.

Database

The API server is the only component that connects with the cluster database that stores all Kubernetes resources. The API server handles client authentication, authorization, and input validation, and it makes changes to the resources, but it doesn't *change* anything; the API server is not responsible for finding a node to start a container on. It stores the resources in the cluster database—nothing more.

Controllers

If you create, update, or delete resources, you're describing how you would like the cluster to look—you're providing the blueprint. Every resource type has a dedicated *controller* that tries to actually change the cluster for you to make it match your description.

This is what happens after you create a deployment resource: the deployment controller picks up the creation event and creates other lower-level Kubernetes resources in response (a ReplicaSet). Every type of Kubernetes resource has a different controller that watches over it, so another controller picks up the lower-level resource, finally resulting in the creation of Pods, and they are scheduled to start on a node.

On every node, a *kubelet* process continuously watches the API server to see if a Pod is scheduled on its node, and as soon as that happens, it starts the containers.

Adding Extensions to Kubernetes

You can define your own custom types of Kubernetes resources and tell the API server about them using a custom resource definition (CRD). You can then start your own controllers that watch for changes in your custom resources and create other built-in Kubernetes resources in response.

This is how Knative is an extension to Kubernetes: it adds new resources to Kubernetes, such as Service,[1] Configuration, and Revision. Knative also starts new controllers that watch these resources. When a new Knative Service comes in, the Knative controllers create and manage a Kubernetes deployment resource under the hood.

Running Knative Serving Locally

Now that I've introduced the major concepts to you, it is time for a hands-on exploration. Before diving in, I want to be very clear about the goal of this exercise. I want to show you how to take a service from Cloud Run to a Knative Serving install on your local machine—completely out of Google Cloud. While this is useful to illustrate the compatibility of Cloud Run and Knative Serving, you should probably not use a local Kubernetes cluster for local development. I show a better way to do that with Docker in Chapter 6.

The various scripts and listings in this chapter can also be found in this repository (*https://oreil.ly/hRN4I*).

Running a Local Kubernetes Cluster

Before I continue, I should warn you: depending on your background and where you are in your learning journey, you might feel a bit lost in this part. You might hear a lot of new terms and concepts. I can't possibly explain every abstraction, but I will do my best to refer you to additional resources along the way.

If you want to run a local Kubernetes cluster on your machine, there are several alternatives. The popular options are Minikube, k3s, and kind. Minikube has been around the longest, is community maintained, and is friendly for beginners. It uses a virtual machine (or a Docker container) to run a single-node Kubernetes cluster. This means you can easily throw everything out and start from scratch with a new cluster, which helps with learning.

---

1 If you are familiar with Kubernetes, you'll know that there is also a `Service` object in Kubernetes. The Knative Service is an entirely different resource with different semantics.

A good overview of available alternatives for running local Kubernetes clusters is in the webinar "Navigating the Sea of Local Kubernetes Clusters" (*https://oreil.ly/ncPdD*) and its accompanying slides (*https://oreil.ly/MVYpG*).

Installing Minikube and kubectl

Your first task is to install Minikube and kubectl, the general-purpose Kubernetes client. You can use gcloud to install both. I know you have gcloud installed, so this is the example I'll run with. If you want to take a different approach, take a look at the installation documentation for kubectl (*https://oreil.ly/PjNYt*) and Minikube (*https://oreil.ly/jEN6k*).

First, make sure you have the most recent version of gcloud:

```
gcloud components update
```

Now install Minikube. This component can take a while to install, especially if you have limited internet bandwidth:

```
gcloud components install minikube
```

When the Minikube install finishes, type **minikube version** to check if the install was successful. It should output minikube version: v1.13.0 (or a higher version). After installing Minikube, you can continue to install kubectl, the Kubernetes client:

```
gcloud components install kubectl
```

To check if the installation succeeded, type **kubectl**: you should see a long list of available commands if you successfully installed the tool.

Starting Your Local Cluster

This command will create a local Kubernetes cluster of one node. Start the cluster:

```
minikube start --kubernetes-version=1.19.2
```

It will either use a local virtual machine or a Docker container to run the Kubernetes node. Using a container to run your Kubernetes node, which runs containers, sounds a lot like the plot of the 2010 science fiction movie *Inception*, in which actors descend through multiple stacked layers of subconsciousness (a "dream in a dream"). However, the mental model of "layers" is incorrect here: containers isolate processes that run next to one another on the same host.

If you are on macOS, you might find that the virtual machine driver is more stable than the Docker driver; some people experience high CPU usage when running the Docker driver. Use this command to delete the Docker-based cluster and choose the virtual machine driver on macOS:

```
minikube delete
minikube start --driver=hyperkit --kubernetes-version=1.19.2
```

When the command finishes (it can take a while), check if it worked:

```
$: minikube status
minikube
type: Control Plane
host: Running
kubelet: Running
apiserver: Running
kubeconfig: Configured
```

Your output should look similar to the following and report that services are running. Minikube will also update your kubectl configuration to connect it to your fresh cluster. This means you can get a list for the internal components that are already running in your cluster using kubectl:

```
$: kubectl get --namespace kube-system pods
NAMESPACE      NAME                                      READY    STATUS
kube-system    coredns-66bff467f8-h9djq                  1/1      Running
kube-system    etcd-minikube                             1/1      Running
kube-system    kube-apiserver-minikube                   1/1      Running
kube-system    kube-controller-manager-minikube          1/1      Running
kube-system    kube-proxy-lwcr2                          1/1      Running
kube-system    kube-scheduler-minikube                   1/1      Running
kube-system    storage-provisioner                       1/1      Running
```

This command tells kubectl to list the core components that are part of the Kubernetes system (the kube-system namespace). If all these pods have the *Running* status, your cluster is good to go.

If you look back at Figure 10-2, you can recognize a few components in this listing: the database is etcd. The API server is kube-apiserver, and the kube-controller-manager runs the built-in Kubernetes controllers.

Install the Knative Operator

Now that you have a Kubernetes cluster running on your local host, you can add Knative Serving to it. The first step is to install the Knative Operator. This is a process that can install Knative Serving for you.

Use kubectl apply to install the operator; it takes a YAML file with Kubernetes resources and submits them to the API server. This is how you install the Knative Operator (as of October 2020). The URL to the operator is very long, which is why I shortened it for you using GitHub's *git.io* URL shortener (*git.io* only redirects to *github.com* URLs):

```
kubectl apply -f https://git.io/JUd0x
```

If you look closely at the output of the command, you will recognize that it adds two custom resources and deploys the `knative-operator`.

You can check that it is running with this command, which lists all deployments:

```
$: kubectl get deployments
NAME                READY   UP-TO-DATE   AVAILABLE
knative-operator    1/1     1            1
```

Your next task is to add the `knative-serving` namespace:

```
$: kubectl create namespace knative-serving
namespace/knative-serving created
```

Starting Minikube Tunnel

In a separate Terminal tab, start the Minikube tunnel and keep it running. This command needs root privileges to create a network path to your cluster, ensuring that you can reach the private IPs on your cluster:

```
minikube tunnel
```

Finally, you are now ready to add the object that describes the Knative Serving extension (Example 10-1). You need to put the object in a YAML file and use `kubectl` `apply` to send it to the API server. The operator then picks up the object and installs Knative Serving for you.

Example 10-1. The contents of knative-serving.yml

```
apiVersion: operator.knative.dev/v1alpha1
kind: KnativeServing
metadata:
 namespace: knative-serving
 name: knative-serving
spec:
 config:
   network:
     ingress.class: "kourier.ingress.networking.knative.dev"
```

Add this listing to a file, call it *knative-serving.yml*, and then send it to the API server using the `apply` command:

```
$: kubectl apply -f knative-serving.yml
knativeserving.operator.knative.dev/knative-serving created
```

The operator should have picked up the resource and installed it for you. Check and wait until the deployments are all complete (all should list `AVAILABLE 1`):

```
$: kubectl get deployment -n knative-serving
NAME               READY   UP-TO-DATE   AVAILABLE   AGE
activator          1/1     1            1           3m48s
autoscaler         1/1     1            1           3m48s
autoscaler-hpa     1/1     1            1           3m44s
controller         1/1     1            1           3m47s
webhook            1/1     1            1           3m47s
```

Installing an HTTP Load Balancer

Incoming requests need to be forwarded to Knative Serving, which means you'll need to install an HTTP load balancer,[2] which acts as the front door to Serving. I picked Kourier for this walkthrough because it is the easiest to set up and route traffic to. Install Kourier v0.17.0 like this:

```
$: kubectl apply -f https://git.io/JUdus
namespace/kourier-system created
service/kourier created
deployment.apps/3scale-kourier-gateway created
deployment.apps/3scale-kourier-control created
clusterrole.rbac.authorization.k8s.io/3scale-kourier created
serviceaccount/3scale-kourier created
clusterrolebinding.rbac.authorization.k8s.io/3scale-kourier created
service/kourier-internal created
service/kourier-control created
configmap/kourier-bootstrap created
```

Kourier exposes an internal `LoadBalancer`, and the Minikube tunnel lets you send traffic to it. Let's find the IP of the `LoadBalancer Ingress`:

```
$: kubectl -n kourier-system describe services kourier
...edited for readability...
LoadBalancer Ingress:    xxx.xxx.xxx.xxx <-- Copy this IP from your listing
...edited for readability...
```

If there is no `LoadBalancer Ingress`, you'll want to check if the Minikube tunnel is running.

---

2 If you're familiar with Kubernetes, you might know this as an *ingress controller*, which is an abstract term if you're not familiar with Kubernetes. This is why I call it an HTTP load balancer.

Configuring DNS

Minikube tunnel adds routes from your host to the internal IPs in the local Kubernetes cluster. Knative uses host-based routing, so you'll need to set up DNS. I'm using the nip.io service. Here's an example (192.168.1.250.nip.io resolves to 192.168.1.250):

```
$: host 192.168.1.250.nip.io
192.168.1.250.nip.io has address 192.168.1.250
```

Edit the *config-domain.yml* file (Example 10-2) to add your LoadBalancer Ingress IP.

Example 10-2. Configuring the domain for your internal services

```
apiVersion: v1
kind: ConfigMap
metadata:
 name: config-domain
 namespace: knative-serving
data:
 xxx.xxx.xxx.xxx.nip.io: ""
```

Replace *xxx.xxx.xxx.xxx* with the IP you copied from the LoadBalancer Ingress, save the file (*config-domain.yml*), and apply it:

```
kubectl apply -f config-domain.yml
```

This last step concludes the setup phase. You now have a fully functioning Knative Serving install running on your local machine. From this point forward, you can deploy your application just as you would deploy to Cloud Run, which is what I'll show you next.

Deploying a Service

In Chapter 3, I showed you how to use a *service.yml* file to deploy a service to Cloud Run. This was the Knative Service resource. Because Cloud Run and Knative use the same resource model, you can deploy the same service definition to Cloud Run and Knative Serving, as shown in Example 10-3.

Example 10-3. Use the service.yml file to deploy the service

```
apiVersion: serving.knative.dev/v1
kind: Service
metadata:
name: hello
spec:
template:
```

```
  spec:
    containers:
    - image: gcr.io/cloud-run-book/inspect
```

Let's start by deploying the service to Knative Serving:

```
$: kubectl apply -f service.yml
service.serving.knative.dev/hello created
```

The service is now ready to invoke. Find the URL:

```
$: kubectl get ksvc
NAME    URL
hello   http://hello.default.xxx.xxx.xxx.xxx.nip.io
```

If you open the URL, you should see the same sample service you deployed in Chapter 2.

Deploying the Same Service to Cloud Run

For good measure, let's deploy the same service to Cloud Run using the exact same YAML file:

```
gcloud beta run services replace service.yml
```

You'll still need to add an IAM policy binding to access it:

```
gcloud run services add-iam-policy-binding hello \
  --member allUsers \
  --role roles/run.invoker
```

If you open the URL, you should see the same page (showing different environment variables).

Alternative API Clients

You might wonder why I'm using gcloud to deploy to Cloud Run and a different client to deploy to Kubernetes if both use the same API. This is mainly because of authentication, which Kubernetes and Google Cloud handle differently. With some hackery, you can make it work. If you are interested in learning more, Salmaan Rashid has written a blog post on the topic (*https://oreil.ly/t6Hpj*).

Another reason you can't use gcloud to manage your local Kubernetes cluster is that gcloud expects Cloud IAM to be available. When you deploy a Cloud Run service with --allow-unauthenticated, gcloud ries to add an IAM policy binding automatically, which fails because Cloud IAM does not exist in your local Kubernetes cluster.

Shutting Down

To shut everything down on your local machine, go back to your Terminal tab with `minikube tunnel` and stop it (stopping it properly will remove the routes).

To delete the single node Kubernetes cluster, run:

```
minikube delete
```

Discussion

This practical exploration gave you an impression of what it means in practice that Cloud Run is based on the open Knative specification. I want to make a few observations and discuss the differences between Knative Serving and Cloud Run.

Serving

Cloud Run provides you with custom domains and automatically obtains and renews TLS certificates (for HTTPS). You can get this to work on Knative, but it requires additional configuration.

Moving from Kubernetes to Cloud Run Is Harder

Knative runs on top of Kubernetes, which means you have access to all other Kubernetes primitives when you're building your app. For example, if you want to schedule a job to run at a certain time, you can use the CronJob resource.

The container runtime (gVisor) on Cloud Run has a few limitations. To give an example, you can't mount NFS volumes. If you use a different container runtime on Kubernetes, you can.

When your container is not handling requests on Cloud Run, it is throttled. This limitation does not exist on Kubernetes.

If you run your application on Knative Serving, you'll have access to the entire Kubernetes ecosystem, with the possibility to install additional tooling and customization. If you want to migrate from Knative Serving to Cloud Run, you're more likely to run into issues than if you move from Cloud Run to Knative Serving.

Service Identity and Authentication

On Cloud Run, you use Cloud IAM to handle service identity and authentication.

On Kubernetes, this topic is an innovative space with multiple approaches. Currently, Istio (*https://oreil.ly/LZdWH*) and Envoy (*https://oreil.ly/M9ztD*) are interesting projects to explore. I don't even know how to provide guidance that ages well—I just want to make you aware of your dependency on Cloud IAM if you use Cloud Run.

Proprietary Managed Services

If you use a proprietary managed service on Google Cloud that doesn't have an open source alternative, you'll need to keep using it when you move your application to a different platform—if that is even possible. Cloud IAM, Firestore, Cloud Tasks, and Cloud Scheduler are examples of services without an open source alternative..

Summary

In this chapter, you learned what Knative Serving is and how Kubernetes works. You installed Minikube and `kubectl` on your local machine and learned how to deploy a service. Kubernetes is of course a big topic, and there are entire books devoted to it. *Kubernetes: Up and Running*, 2nd Edition, by Brendan Burns, Joe Beda, and Kelsey Hightower (O'Reilly, 2019) is a good starting point if you decide to dig deeper.

You might never need to move away from Google Cloud, but if you do, this chapter will have started your thinking process about how to approach that migration. Vendor lock-in is always a concern, so it's worth knowing what your options are.

Throughout this book, you've come to understand what makes Cloud Run a unique container platform and how to leverage its features to design, build, and deploy serverless apps that work efficiently and reliably. Google's offerings are always changing and growing, so be sure to consult the relevant documentation as you begin.

I hope that what you've learned here provides you with a great start. Good luck on your journey!

Index

A

access management (see security)
allUsers, 82
    Cloud Run Invoker role, 82
    policy binding with Cloud Run Invoker, 85
Ansible, 114
Apache and PHP-FPM, 28
App Engine
    about, 5, 7
    Buildpacks for container image, 50
    Cloud Run versus, 30-32
applications
    database tier, 57
    running a container, 37
    serverless (see serverless applications)
    shutdown SIGTERM signal, 22
        (see also shutdown)
    web-based application definition, 1
Artifact Registry
    about, 33, 44-46
    docker repository, 45
    enabling in project, 45
    ko for Go containers, 47
    pushing container image to, 46
authentication
    Cloud SQL Proxy Server, 58, 60
    container image credentials, 46
    Kubernetes
        API server, 151
        Cloud Run versus, 159
    sending authenticated requests
        about, 88
        Google Frontend latency, 92
        ID token, 89

        ID token validity, 90
        private service, 88
        programmatically, 90
    service accounts, 85
        default service account avoided, 86, 96
automation for infrastructure management, 113
autoscaler, 26
    concurrency setting and, 27
    load balancer and, 24
    maximum number of containers, 26
    throttled containers versus cold starts, 27
availability, 3

B

backend URL in environment variable, 93
bash shell container image, 34
    overriding default command, 35
Beda, Joe, 151, 160
beginning (see getting started)
Borg, 5, 8
Buildpacks, 31, 49
Burns, Brendan, 151, 160

C

carbon neutrality of Google Cloud, 6
CentOS Linux distribution, 43
child processes, 39
CLI (see gcloud command line interface)
Cloud
    about, 1
    Google account, 82
    projects on, 15
    region of deployment, 17
        available services per, 18

serverless products on, 7
sustainability, 6
Cloud Build
    about, 50
    advanced builds, 51
    container deployment, 63
    remote docker build, 51
    running arbitrary programs, 53
    version control trigger, 53
    YAML build configuration file, 51
Cloud Client Libraries, 85
Cloud Console mobile app, 14
Cloud Error Reporting, 131
    panic in Cloud Logging, 135
Cloud Functions, 7
    Buildpacks for container image, 50
    Cloud Run versus, 29, 30
Cloud IAM (Identity and Access Management)
    about, 81
        policy binding, 82-85
        roles, 81
        service accounts, 82
            (see also service accounts)
    Cloud SQL Proxy Server, 58, 60
    private Cloud Run service, 88
    proprietary managed service, 160
    serverless infrastructure, 113
    Terraform access policy example, 124
Cloud Logging
    about, 129
        Cloud Operations Suite, 131
    Cloud Run information captured, 129
    Stackdriver as prior name, 134
    structured logs
        benefits, 144
        client libraries, 134
        JSON logs with extra fields, 133
        JSON message structure, 134
        request context, 137-138
        trace context, 139-143
        viewing trace context, 143
    terminal interface, 130
    web console link to, 130
Cloud Monitoring
    about, 131
    Cloud SQL in production, 69
    log-based metrics, 143
Cloud Run
    about, 1, 7, 8
    autoscaler, 26
    cold starts, 27
    concurrency setting, 27
    concurrent request limit, 26
    container life cycle, 22
    container port number, 16, 22
    CPU throttling, 24
    developer workflow, 8, 31
    disposable containers, 27, 71, 79
    in-memory filesystem, 28
    key points, 28
    load balancer and autoscaler, 24
    memory limits, 28, 93
    pricing, 10, 24, 27
    ready for requests, 28
    request driven, 13
    revisions, 20
    task scheduling and throttling, 24
    App Engine versus, 30-32
    client authentication versus Kubernetes, 158
    Cloud Functions versus, 29, 30
    Cloud SQL
        connecting to, 61, 63
        disabling direct connection, 62
    configuration, 10
    container image, 8
    cost model, 4, 10
        always-free tier, 14
        concerns about, 11
        costs, 14
    deployments, 10
        (see also deployments)
    developer workflow, 8
    getting started
        always-free tier, 14
        costs, 14
        deploying first service, 16-21, 35
        Google Cloud account, 13
        Google Cloud projects, 15, 45
        installing beta component, 16
        installing SDK, 15
        interacting with, 14
        region and available services, 18
        region of deployment, 17
    HTTPS serving, 9
        endpoint on deployment, 16, 18
        internal services that are not public, 9
    identity and authentication, 9
    Invoker role, 82

add to project and service, 84
Knative compatibility, 147, 148
    deploying service with same YAML file,
        158
    differences between, 159
    separate from Knative, 148
Kubernetes to Cloud Run, 159
logging
    about, 10
    finding invisible logs, 131
    information captured, 129
    plain text logs, 132
        (see also structured logging)
    terminal interface, 130
    viewing logs in web console, 130
microservices support, 9
monitoring, 10
other products versus, 29-32
portability of, 12, 147
replace command, 48
scalability, 4, 9
    hyper-scalability concerns, 11, 55, 65
    limiting concurrency, 65-69
self-healing, 9
serverless
    concerns about, 10-12
    FaaS versus, 5
    serverless infrastructure, 113
service, 8
session affinity, 78
source-based workflow, 31
task scheduling, 99, 100
    (see also task scheduling)
    maximum request duration, 101
VPC connector for private IPs, 74
    (see also Virtual Private Cloud (VPC)
        network)
Cloud Scheduler, 7
Cloud SQL
    about, 7, 55, 78
    Cloud SQL Client role, 82
    database servers supported, 55, 57
    demo application
        about, 55
        Cloud Run connected to, 61, 63
        Cloud Run direct connection disabled,
          62
        Cloud SQL Client, 59, 60
        Cloud SQL enabled, 57

Cloud SQL instance, 57
Cloud SQL instance costs, 58
Cloud SQL Proxy, 58, 60
    connection string, 64
    database servers, 57
    deploying, 63
    MySQL connection, 59
    MySQL installation, 59
    public and private IP, 64
    schema, 60
    security, 60
    Todo-Backend, 56
limiting concurrency
    about, 65
    external connection pooling, 68
    internal connection pooling, 68
    real-world example, 69
    resource contention, 67
    scaling boundaries, 68
    transaction concurrency, 65
machine type (tier), 57
not serverless, 7, 58
production
    automatic storage increase, 69
    high availability, 69
    monitoring, 69
    resilient against short downtimes, 70
service level agreement, 78
shutdown
    instance costs, 58
    instances deleted, 70
    instances listed, 70
Cloud Storage, 7
Cloud Functions as glue, 29
Cloud Tasks
    about, 7, 99
    about queue, 101
    considerations
        alternatives, 108
        local development, 108
        request delivered twice, 107
    demo application
        about, 101
        Client library to schedule task, 103
        connecting to task queue, 103
        container images built, 101
        ID token added automatically, 104
        queue creation, 102
        scheduling a task, 103

service accounts created, 102
task-app service deployed, 103
testing app, 105
worker service connected, 105
worker service deployed, 102
emulator (third party), 108
Enqueuer role, 82
maximum request duration, 101
queue configuration
rate limiting, 106
retry configuration, 105
viewing and updating, 107
Cloud Trace, 131
configuring in a Go app, 143
Cloud Workflows, 108
clusters in Kubernetes, 149
API server connecting with database, 151
resource controllers, 151
cold starts, 27
command line interface (see gcloud command
line interface)
Compute Engine, 5
concurrent request limit, 26
concurrency setting, 26, 27
real-world example, 69
resource contention, 67
scaling boundaries, 68
transaction concurrency, 65
configuration
about Cloud Run, 10
concurrency setting, 26, 27
container configuration, 93
container image configuration, 36
minimum instances setting, 27
revisions, 20
service configuration, 20
YAML configuration of service, 48
connection pooling
external, 68
internal, 68
container registry, 44
Cloud Build remote docker build, 51
Container Security (book; Rice), 40
containers
about Cloud Run
memory limits, 28, 93
request driven, 13
autoscaler, 24, 26
maximum number of containers, 26

minimum instances setting, 27
Borg, 5, 8
building
additional tooling installed, 42
Buildpacks, 31, 49
Cloud Build, 50
distroless for small containers, 43
Dockerfile instructions, 41
Jib for Java containers, 49
ko for Go containers, 47-48
smaller is better, 43
Visual Studio Code Remote Containers
extension, 95
with Docker, 40-44
without Dockerfile, 46-50
concurrent request limit, 26
concurrency setting, 26, 27
consecutive error responses, 28
container image
Artifact Registry, 33, 44-46
bash shell, 34
Cloud Run, 9
Cloud Tasks demo app, 101
contents of, 36
definition, 8, 16, 34, 36
deploying first service, 16-21, 35
deploying new version, 19
deploying requiring, 40
image configuration, 36
image URL tag, 45
revisions, 20
CPU throttling (see CPU throttling)
definitions, 16
disposable, 27, 71, 79
Knative Serving same, 148
exploring
bash shell, 34
Docker Desktop installation, 34
overriding default command, 35
running a server, 35
functions as a service versus, 5
isolation of, 38, 39
Kubernetes
API server, 151
node running in, 153
resources, 151
life cycle, 22
shutdown, 22
Linux kernel, 37

load balancer, 24
logging via output streams, 130
network stack, 35
    virtual ethernet interface, 38
port number, 16, 22
portability of Cloud Run, 12
session affinity, 78
shutdown, 22
source-based versus, 31
starting a container, 39
controllers for Kubernetes resources, 151
cookies
    session affinity, 78
    session ID, 72
cost model
    Cloud account to get started, 13
        always-free tier, 14
        costs, 14
    Cloud Run, 10
        CPU throttling, 24
        throttled containers, 27
    Cloud SQL instance, 58
        region, 57
    example services from book, 54
    Memorystore instance costs, 74, 78
    requests with invalid ID tokens, 90
    serverless applications, 4
        concerns about, 11
    VPC Connector, 76
CPU throttling, 24
    Knative versus Cloud Run, 159
    shutdown, 22
    task scheduling and, 24, 99
    throttled containers versus cold starts, 27
credentials
    container images, 46
    gcloud managing, 116
crzerolog package for request trace IDs, 137
    trace ID forwarding, 140
custom resource definitions (CRDs; Kubernetes), 152

D
data storage
    Cloud SQL automatic increase, 69
    containers disposable, 27, 71, 79
        Knative Serving same, 148
    databases (see Cloud SQL)
    in-memory filesystem, 28

machine type (tier), 57
    separation of compute and storage, 11
    Storage Object Admin role, 82
database servers
    Cloud SQL instance, 57
    external connection pooling, 68
    internal connection pooling, 68
    scaling boundaries, 68
    supported by Cloud SQL, 55, 57
    transaction concurrency, 65
        resource contention, 67
Debian Linux distribution, 43
default service account avoided, 86, 96
deployments
    about Cloud Run, 10
    Artifact Registry container image, 46
    Cloud Functions, 29
    Cloud SQL demo application, 63
    container image required for, 40
    deploying first service
        container image, 16
        deploying container image, 16
        deploying new version, 19
        Docker to run, 35
        HTTPS endpoint, 16, 18
        region, 17
        revisions, 20
        viewing in web console, 18
    Knative Serving, 157
        Cloud Run with same YAML file, 158
    Kubernetes resource, 151
        resource controllers, 151
    Memorystore demo app, 77
    private service, 88
    region, 17
        Artifact Registry, 45
        deploying Cloud SQL demo, 63
        deploying first service, 17
    serverless versus FaaS, 5
    service deployment YAML files, 48, 157
    smaller is better, 43
    Terraform
        execution plan, 120
        execution plan applied, 121
developer workflow, 8
disposable containers, 27, 71, 79
    Knative Serving same, 148
distributed tracing, 139-143
    book on distributed tracing, 139

Cloud Trace, 131, 143
    forwarding trace ID, 139
    incoming requests with trace ID, 141
    outgoing requests with request context, 141
    viewing trace context in Cloud Logging, 143
Distributed Tracing in Practice (book; Parker,
    Spoonhower, Mace, Sigelman, and Isaacs),
    139
distroless for small containers, 43
    Java containers, 49
DNS configuration, 157
Docker
    bash shell container image, 34
    building a container, 40-44
        Cloud Build remote docker build, 51
        distroless for small containers, 43
        docker build, 41
        installing additional tooling, 42
        smaller is better, 43
    Dockerfiles
        about, 40
        building a container, 41
        distroless for small containers, 43
        installing additional tooling, 42
    ethernet interface, 38
    installation of Docker Desktop, 34
    for local development, not Knative, 147, 152
    running first deployed service, 35
    starting a container, 39
    stopping with Ctrl-C, 35
Docker Compose
    about, 93
    Cloud SQL demo, 57
    demo SQL application
        about, 92
        custom service accounts added, 96
        default service account, 96
        deploying on Cloud Run, 95
        embedded read-only SQL database, 93
        Frontend configuration update, 96
        IAM policy binding, 96
        running locally, 93
        selective rebuild and restart, 94
        Visual Studio Code Remote Containers
            extension, 95
    environment variables
        backend URL, 93
        connection strings, 64
    for local development, not Knative, 147, 152

    selective rebuild and restart, 94
    downtime resilience, 70

E
environment variables
    backend URL, 93
    connection strings, 64
    container image URL tag, 45
    image configuration, 36
    KO_DOCKER_REPO, 47
    service configuration, 20
    Terraform parameters, 118
environmental sustainability of Cloud, 6
Envoy, 159
Events for Cloud Run, 7
events from Cloud products, 9

F
FaaS (functions as a service), 5
filesystem
    bash shell container image, 35
    Linux kernel, 37, 38
    in memory, 28
    starting a container, 39
    Storage Object Admin role, 82
    UNIX Domain Socket for listening, 61, 63
        connection string, 64
Firestore
    about, 7, 78
    moving app to different platform, 160
    service level agreement, 78
Frontend Server (see Google Frontend Server)
functions as a service (FaaS), 5
Furuyama, Yuki, 137

G
gcloud command line interface
    about, 14
    Cloud account to get started, 13
    Cloud Build enabled, 50
    Cloud Logging, 130
    Cloud SQL
        deploying demo application, 63
        enabling, 57
        instance created, 57
        instances deleted, 70
        instances listed, 70
        MySQL connection, 59

proxy, 59
schema, 60
security, 60
Cloud Tasks demo
    connecting to task queue, 103
    container images built, 101
    queue creation, 102
    service accounts created, 102
    task-app service deployed, 103
    worker service connected, 105
    worker service deployed, 102
Cloud Tasks queue configuration, 107
credentials, 116
deleting services, 54
ID token, 89
kubectl installation, 153
Memorystore
    deploying demo app, 77
    enabling, 73
    instance creation, 74
    shutting down, 80
    VPC connector, 76
    VPC connectors active, 80
Minikube installation, 153
role permissions listed, 86
services listed, 54
updating to latest version, 153
YAML configuration of service, 48
getting started
    about Cloud Run, 28
        autoscaler, 26
        cold starts, 27
        concurrency setting, 27
        concurrent request limit, 26
        container life cycle, 22
        CPU throttling, 24
        disposable containers, 27, 71, 79
        load balancer and autoscaler, 24
        memory limits, 28
        ready for requests, 28
        task scheduling and throttling, 24
    deploying first service, 16-21
        container image, 16
        deploying container image, 16
        deploying new version, 19
        Docker to run, 35
        HTTPS endpoint, 16, 18
        region, 17
        region and available services, 18

revisions, 20
viewing in web console, 18
Google Cloud account, 13, 14
    always-free tier, 14
Google Cloud projects, 15
    container image URL tag, 45
interacting with Cloud Run, 14
introduction to concepts (see introduction)
SDK installation, 15
    beta component installation, 16
Terraform Hello World, 116-122
Go language
    Cloud Trace configuration, 143
    crzerolog package for request trace IDs, 137
        trace ID forwarding, 140
    Go app into container image, 40
        distroless for small containers, 43
        Dockerfile instructions, 41
        ko for Go containers, 47-48
        smaller is better, 43
    Goroutine background threads, 108
    ID token in HTTP header via idtoken, 90
        request context to outgoing request, 141
        trace ID compatibility, 141
        trace ID forwarding, 140
    panic function, 135
    why use, xviii
    zerolog package, 134
Google
    Borg
        Cloud Run on top of, 8
        paper on, 5
    Cloud
        about, 1, 5
        account for Cloud Run, 13
        account for logging in to, 82
        details (see Cloud)
        logging (see Cloud Logging)
    Cloud Client Libraries, 85
    Cloud Run
        about, 1
        cost model, 4, 14
        details (see Cloud Run)
        other products versus, 29-32
        session affinity, 79
    Frontend Server (see Google Frontend
        Server)
    Go language, xviii
        (see also Go language)

Google account, 82
Google Frontend Server
    about, 91
    demo application
        about, 92
        custom service accounts added, 96
        default service account, 96
        deploying on Cloud Run, 95
        embedded read-only SQL database, 93
        Frontend configuration update, 96
        IAM policy binding, 96
        running locally, 93
        selective rebuild and restart, 94
        Visual Studio Code Remote Containers
            extension, 95
    latency, 92
    request trace IDs for logging, 137
        distributed tracing, 140
GraalVM (Oracle), 49

H

HashiCorp Configuration Language (HCL),
    119
high availability, 69
Hightower, Kelsey, 151, 160
HTTP
    about book usage of term, 2
    consecutive server error responses, 28
    container port number, 16
    CPU throttling, 24
    evolution explained, 2
    ID token in header, 90
    load balancer installation, 156
    requests (see requests)
    scaling boundary of Cloud Run service, 68
    sessions (see sessions)
HTTP 429 error, 26
HTTP 503 errors, 24
HTTPS
    about Cloud Run, 9
        internal services that are not public, 9
    endpoint on deployment
        about, 18
        first container image deployment, 16
    Frontend server, 91
        latency, 92
    Knative versus Cloud Run, 159
    web-based application definition, 1
hyper-scalability concerns, 11, 55, 65

I

ID tokens
    about, 89
    Cloud Tasks, 104
    gcloud printing, 89
        utility to parse, 89
    HTTP headers passing, 90
    validity of, 90
identity
    about, 58
    about Cloud Run, 9, 58
    authentication (see authentication)
    Cloud IAM, 58
        Cloud SQL Proxy Server, 58, 60
    HTTP sessions, 72
    ID tokens, 89
    Kubernetes versus Cloud Run, 159
    roles and, 58
        Cloud IAM, 81
        Cloud SQL Client, 59, 60
        default service account avoided, 86, 96
        listing permissions of roles, 86
        policy binding, 82-85
    service accounts, 58, 85
        (see also service accounts)
    user ID of image configuration, 36
infrastructure
    about, 111
    Borg paper, 5
    serverless, 2, 113
infrastructure as code (IaC)
    about, 111
    how it works, 113
    Terraform tool (see Terraform)
    when not to use, 114
    why use, 112
ingress controller installation, 156
instance-oriented versus request-oriented, 31
introduction
    Cloud, 1, 5
    Cloud Run
        about, 1, 7, 8
        configuration, 10
        container image, 8
        cost model, 4, 10, 11
        deployments, 10
        developer workflow, 8
        HTTPS serving, 9
        identity and authentication, 9

microservices support, 9
monitoring and logging, 10
portability of, 12, 147
scalability, 4, 9, 11
self-healing, 9
serverless, 5
serverless concerns, 10-12
service, 8
Go language, xviii
(see also Go language)
serverless applications
autoscalable, 3
Cloud products, 7
Cloud Run versus others, 29-32
concerns about, 10-12
cost model, 4, 11
definition of applications, 1
definition of serverless, 2
functions as a service versus, 5
infrastructure, 2, 113
open source compatibility, 7, 12
trouble can be trouble, 11
Isaacs, Rebecca, 139
Istio, 159

J

Java
containers via Jib, 49
distroless for smaller containers, 49
Micronaut for GraalVM, 49
Oracle GraalVM, 49
Quarkus, 49
Jib for Java containers, 49

K

Kerrisk, Michael, 38
Knative Operator
installation, 154
Knative Serving installation, 155
Knative Serving
about, 148
disposable containers, 148
Kubernetes extension, 152
Cloud Run compatibility, 147, 148
deploying with same YAML file, 158
differences between, 159
separate from Knative Serving, 148
host-based routing, 157
Kubernetes (see Kubernetes)

local development
about, 152
about Minikube, 152
deploying a service, 157
DNS configuration, 157
Docker for, 147, 152
HTTP load balancer, 156
Knative Operator installation, 154
Knative Serving installation, 155
Knative Serving namespace, 155
Kubernetes local cluster, 152
Kubernetes local cluster started, 153
Minikube installation, 153
Minikube tunnel started, 155
repository URL, 152
shutting down, 159
portability of Cloud Run, 12, 147
session affinity, 79
specification for YAML configuration, 48
ko for Go containers, 47-48
documentation, 47
Kourier load balancer, 156
kubectl
about, 150
installation, 153
internal components list, 154
Knative Operator installation, 154
Knative Serving installation, 155
Knative Serving namespace, 155
Minikube configuring, 154
Kubernetes
about, 149
resources, 151
adding extensions to, 152
Knative as, 152
API server, 150
cluster database connection point, 151
custom resource definitions, 152
book on Kubernetes, 151, 160
client authentication versus Cloud Run, 158
clusters, 149
API server connecting with, 151
resource controllers, 151
CPU throttling nonexistent, 159
deployment resource, 151
resource controllers, 151
ingress controller installation, 156
ko for Go containers, 47
kubectl

about, 150
    installation, 153
    internal components list, 154
    Knative Operator installation, 154
    Knative Serving installation, 155
    Knative Serving namespace, 155
    Minikube configuring, 154
local cluster, 152
    about Minikube, 152
    deleting, 159
    Minikube installation, 153
    resource for learning, 153
    starting, 153
moving to Cloud Run, 159
Pods, 151
    resource controllers, 151
portability of Cloud Run, 12, 147
resources
    API server as connection point, 151
    controllers, 151
    custom resource definitions, 152
    ReplicaSets, 151
Kubernetes: Up and Running (book; Burns;
    Beda, and Hightower), 151, 160

L

latency
    Cloud SQL instance region, 57
    Google Frontend, 92
    Memorystore versus Firestore, 78
    separation of compute and storage, 11
least privilege principle, 81
Linux kernel, 37
    container isolation, 38
Linux Programming Interface (book; Kerrisk),
    38
load balancer
    autoscaler and, 24
    installation, 156
locks and resource contention, 67
log levels, 134
    Panic, 135
        capturing, 135
logging
    Cloud Run
        about, 10
        finding invisible logs, 131
        information captured, 129
        terminal interface, 130

        viewing logs in web console, 130
    container output streams for, 130
    plain text logs, 132
    structured logging, 129
        (see also structured logging)
    terminal interface, 130
    web console Logs tab, 18, 130

M

Mace, Jonathan, 139
machine type (tier)
    Cloud SQL instance, 57
    Memorystore instance, 74
members
    description of, 82
    policy binding, 82
        adding to a project, 83
        adding to a resource, 84
memory limits, 28, 93
Memorystore
    about, 71, 78
    deploying app, 77
    enabling in project, 73
    instance costs, 74, 78
    instance creation, 74
        shutting down, 80
    service level agreement, 78
    shutting down, 80
    VPC connector
        about, 74-76
        costs, 76, 80
        creating, 76
        deleting, 80
        private IP, 74, 77
metadata in logs (see structured logging)
Micronaut for GraalVM, 49
microservices support, 9
Minikube
    about, 152
    deleting Kubernetes cluster, 159
    installing, 153
    kubectl configuration, 154
    macOS VM driver, 153
    shutting down, 159
    status, 154
    tunnel, 155
minimum instances setting, 27
mobile app for Cloud Console, 14
monitoring

about Cloud Run, 10
Cloud Monitoring
    about, 131
    Cloud SQL in production, 69
    log-based metrics, 143
Cloud SQL in production, 69
MySQL
    Cloud SQL supporting, 55
    demo Cloud SQL application
        about, 55
        Cloud SQL instance, 57
        Cloud SQL Proxy, 59, 60
        schema, 60
        securing default user, 60
    installation, 59

N

namespace
    container image, 35
    Knative Serving, 155
network stack of containers, 35
    virtual ethernet interface, 38
NGINX and PHP-FPM, 28

O

Object Admin role, 82
open source compatibility
    Cloud, 7, 12
    Cloud IAM proprietary, 160
    vendor lock-in and, 12
OpenCensus, 141
Operations Suite on Google Cloud, 131
Oracle GraalVM, 49
    Micronaut for GraalVM, 49

P

Panic log level, 135
    capturing panics, 135
Parker, Austin, 139
pay-per-use cost model, 4, 10
    (see also cost model)
performance of tier, 57
permissions
    Cloud SQL, 58
    Kubernetes API server, 151
    private service, 88
    roles in Cloud IAM, 81
    service accounts, 85

default service account avoided, 86, 96
PHP-FPM and NGINX, 28
ping from bash container image, 35
Pods, 151
    resource controllers, 151
Pokémon demo application
    Cloud Monitoring chart, 143
    JSON log, 132
    repository URL, 132
    zerolog package in Go, 134
policy bindings, 82
    adding to a project, 83
    adding to a resource, 84
    serverless infrastructure, 113
portability of Cloud Run, 12, 147
    definition of portability, 147
ports
    8080 for containers, 16, 22
    cold starts, 27
    container readiness, 28
    Docker localhost connecting to, 35
    frontend container, 94
    UNIX Domain Socket instead, 61, 63
pricing (see cost model)
principle of least privilege, 10
private IP
    Cloud SQL instance, 64
    Memorystore instance, 74, 113
    public versus, 64
    Virtual Private Cloud network, 74
processes
    containers isolating, 153
    invisible logs and, 131
    running container program, 37, 39
        kernel control of environment, 38
    shutdown, 22
production
    Cloud SQL
        automatic storage increase, 69
        high availability, 69
        monitoring, 69
        resilient against short downtimes, 70
        security, 61
    Project Editor role, 86
program in container image, 37
Project Editor role, 86
Pub/Sub, 7
    queue for HTTP requests, 108
public IP versus private, 64

Q
Quarkus, 49

R
rate limiting configuration, 106
Redis
    about, 71, 77
    creating Memorystore instance, 73
    enabling in project, 73
    instance creation, 74
    serverless infrastructure, 113
    VPC connector
        about, 74-76
        costs, 76, 80
        creating, 76
        deleting, 80
        Memorystore private IP, 74
region of deployment
    about, 17
        same throughout book, 45
    Artifact Registry, 45
    Cloud available services, 18
        Knative Serving when no presence, 148
    Cloud SQL instance, 57, 63
    deploying first service, 17
relational databases
    Cloud SQL not serverless, 7, 58
        (see also Cloud SQL)
    demo application, 92
    serverless missing, 7
replace command of Cloud Run, 48
repository for Artifact Registry, 45
requests
    authenticated
        about, 88
        Google Frontend latency, 92
        Google Frontend server, 91
        ID token, 89
        ID token validity, 90
        private service, 88
        programmatically calling, 90
    Cloud Run request driven, 13
    cold starts, 27
    concurrent request limit, 26
    instance-oriented versus, 31
    logging request trace IDs, 137-138
        distributed tracing, 139-143
    minimum instances setting, 27
    Pub/Sub as queue for, 108

sent if container ready, 28
task scheduling
    about, 99
    background threads, 108
    Cloud Tasks demo, 101
        (see also Cloud Tasks)
    CPU throttling and, 24
    ID token, 104
    maximum request duration, 101
    queue, 101
    retry configuration, 105
    success definition, 101
resource contention, 67
resources
    Cloud definition, 111
        Knative Serving same model, 148
    Cloud Foundation Fabric, 126
    Kubernetes, 151
        API server as connection point, 151
        controllers, 151
        custom resource definitions, 152
        Knative as extension, 152
        ReplicaSets, 151
    Terraform
        declarative configuration language, 112
        integration with Cloud, 118, 126
resources for learning
    book downloads, xx
    book errata, xxi
    Cloud
        region and available services, 18
        Terraform resources, 118, 126
    Cloud IAM roles, 82
    Cloud Logging JSON message structure, 134
    Cloud Trace configuration in Go app, 143
    container fundamentals book, 40
    Distributed Tracing in Practice book, 139
    distroless project, 44
    external connection pooling, 68
    HTTP evolution overview, 2
    ko documentation, 47
    Kubernetes
        book on Kubernetes, 151, 160
        client authentication versus gcloud, 158
        local clusters, 153
    Linux OS fundamentals book, 38
    MySQL installation, 59
    Terraform
        additional information, 126

Cloud resources, 118, 126
    documentation, 115
  web console URL, 18, 130
retry configuration, 105
revisions
  about Cloud Run, 20
  about Knative Serving, 148
  cold starts, 27
  container life cycle, 22
Rice, Liz, 40
roles and identity, 58
  Cloud IAM, 81
  Cloud SQL Client, 59, 60
  default service account avoided, 86, 96
  listing permissions of roles, 86
  policy binding, 82
    adding to a project, 83
    adding to a resource, 84

S

scalability
  about Cloud Run, 9
  about Knative Serving, 148
  about serverless applications, 3
  autoscaler, 26
    load balancer and, 24
    maximum number of containers, 26
  Cloud SQL bottlenecks, 55
  cost uncertainties, 11
  CPU-intensive background task, 24
  hyper-scalability concerns, 11, 55, 65
  load balancer and autoscaler, 24
  microservices support and, 9
  VPC connector throughput, 76
scaling boundaries, 68
schema for Cloud SQL, 60
SDK installation, 15
  authentication, 15
  beta component installation, 16
security
  authentication (see authentication)
  Cloud SQL
    Cloud Run direct connection, 62
    Cloud SQL Proxy, 58, 60
    default user, 60
    instance firewall, 60
    production system, 61
    public and private IP, 64
  HTTP sessions, 73

identity (see identity)
  least privilege principle, 81
  small container images and, 43
  structured logging metadata, 135
  Terraform
    service account key, 115
    state file, 122
self-healing, 9
separation of compute and storage, 11
serverless applications
  autoscalable, 3
  Cloud products, 7
  Cloud Run versus others, 29-32
  concerns about, 10-12
  cost model, 4
    concerns about, 11
  definition of applications, 1
  definition of serverless, 2
  functions as a service versus, 5
  infrastructure, 2, 113
  open source compatibility, 7, 12
  trouble can be trouble, 11
service accounts
  about, 58, 82
  create new service account, 87
    authentication demo, 96
    Cloud Tasks demo, 102
  permissions, 85
    create new service account, 87
    default service account avoided, 86, 96
service level agreements (SLAs), 78
  Cloud SQL, 78
  Firestore, 78
  Memorystore, 78
services
  about Cloud Run, 8
  about service accounts, 85
    (see also service accounts)
  Cloud Run Invoker role, 82, 82
    add to project and service, 84
  Cloud Task, 100
  least privilege principle, 81
  private service, 88
    ID token in HTTP header, 90
  programmatically calling, 90
sessions
  about, 71
  how they work, 72
  security, 73

session affinity, 78, 78
session data
    disposable containers, 71, 79
    examples of, 71
    HTTP session description, 72
    Memorystore, 71, 72, 73-77
    Redis for persistence, 71
    session affinity not for, 79
    session stores, 77
    stateless APIs, 71
shutdown
    application response, 22
    Cloud SQL instances
        costs, 58
        deleted, 70
        listing, 70
    container life cycle, 22
    example services from book, 54
    Kubernetes cluster deleted, 159
    Memorystore instance, 80
    Minikube tunnel, 159
    services deleted, 54
    services listed, 54
    SIGTERM warning, 22
    VPC connector, 80
Sigelman, Ben, 139
SIGTERM signal on shutdown, 22
source-based versus containers, 31
Spoonhower, Daniel, 139
SQLite database, 93
SSL/TLS for Cloud SQL connection, 62
Stackdriver becoming Cloud Logging, 134
stateless APIs, 71
Storage Object Admin role, 82
structured logging
    about, 129, 132
        benefits, 144
    Cloud Logging
        about, 134
        JSON message structure, 134
        log levels, 134
        Panic, 135
        readable logs via ConsoleWriter, 137
        request context, 137-138
        trace context, 139-143
    demo application
        Cloud Monitoring chart, 143
        JSON log, 132
        repository URL, 132
    zerolog package in Go, 134
    JSON logs into Cloud Logging, 133
    security and metadata, 135
sustainability of Google Cloud, 6

T

task scheduling
    about, 99
    about Cloud Tasks, 99
        (see also Cloud Tasks)
    Cloud Tasks Enqueuer role, 82
    CPU throttling and, 24, 99
Terraform (HashiCorp)
    about, 111, 115
    about infrastructure as code, 111
        how it works, 113
        when not to use, 114
        why use, 112
    about serverless infrastructure, 113
    Cloud resources, 118, 126
    declarative configuration language, 119
        about, 112, 115
    documentation, 115
    file names, 120
    Hello World example, 116-122
        deployment plan, 120
        deployment plan applied, 121
        initializing Terraform, 117
        input variables, 121
        main.tf file, 116
        provider plug-in, 117
        provider reference, 117
        resource declaration, 118
        source code URL, 116
        state file, 122
        variables as parameters, 118
    installing, 115
        security of service account, 115
    local names, 119
    project ID, 121
    providers, 117
    resources for learning, 126
        Cloud, 118
        Cloud resources, 126
        documentation, 115
    security
        key, 115
        state file, 122
    state file, 122

workflow, 122-126
    access policy change example, 124
    dependencies as references, 125
throttling (see CPU throttling)
tier
    Cloud SQL instance, 57
    Memorystore instance, 74
Tippett, Chris, 68
TLS certificate renewal, 159
Todo-Backend, 56
tracing
    distributed tracing, 139-143
        book on distributed tracing, 139
        Cloud Trace, 131, 143
        forwarding trace ID, 139
        incoming requests with trace ID, 141
        outgoing requests with request context, 141
        viewing trace context in Cloud Logging, 143
    request trace IDs for logging, 137
        crzerolog package for, 137
transaction concurrency, 65
    resource contention, 67

U

Ubuntu Linux distribution, 43
UNIX Domain Socket for listening, 61, 63
    connection string, 64
update command, 20
    revisions, 20
upgrading programs
    Cloud Build version control trigger, 53
    deploying new version, 19
    gcloud update, 153
user ID of image configuration, 36

V

vendor tie-in
    Cloud SQL database engine support, 55
    open source compatibility, 7, 12
    trouble can be trouble, 11
versions
    Cloud Build version control, 53
    deploying new version, 19
    infrastructure as code version control, 112
    Terraform main.tf file, 116

Virtual Private Cloud (VPC) network
    about, 74
    private IP, 64, 74
    VPC connector
        about, 64, 71, 74-76
        costs, 76, 80
        creating, 76
        deleting, 80
        deploying demo app, 77
        listing active connectors, 80
        private IP, 74, 77
        scaling on throughput, 76
        serverless infrastructure, 113
Visual Studio Code Remote Containers extension, 95

W

web console (Cloud Run)
    interacting with Cloud Run, 14
    link to Cloud Logging, 130
    Logs tab, 18, 130
    services viewed on, 18
    URL, 18, 130
web-based applications definition, 1
    (see also applications)
working directory, 36

Y

YAML files
    Cloud Build configuration, 51
    configuration of service, 48
    container configuration, 64, 93
    Knative Serving API specification, 48
    Knative Serving installation, 155
    service deployment, 48, 157, 158
YourSurprise concurrency example, 69

Z

zerolog package in Go
    about, 134
    ConsoleWriter for readable logs, 137
    crzerolog for request trace IDs, 137
        trace ID forwarding, 140
    log levels, 134
        Panic, 135

About the Author

Wietse Venema is a software engineer. If he's not training teams to build scalable and reliable software, he's figuring out how things work so he can be a better engineer and teacher. He works at Binx.io to help companies build what's next in the public cloud.

He's proud to be the name twin (not related) of the famous Wietse Venema, who created Postfix.

Colophon

The animal on the cover of *Building Serverless Applications with Google Cloud Run* is a Eurasian spoonbill (*Platalea leucorodia*). The spoonbill is a Palearctic species found throughout Eurasia and North Africa. The Netherlands, where the author lives, still has a sizeable population. They are wading birds that inhabit shallow wetlands.

Adult spoonbills have white feathers with a yellow breast patch, black legs, and a black bill with a yellow tip. Outside of the breeding season, spoonbills live and migrate in flocks of up to one hundred individuals. Their diet consists of aquatic invertebrates and crustaceans. They are usually silent.

Spoonbill habitat is threatened by destruction and pollution; however, its conservation status is least concern. Many of the animals on O'Reilly covers are endangered; all of them are important to the world.

The cover illustration is by Karen Montgomery, based on a black and white engraving from *Lydekker's Royal Natural History*. The cover fonts are Gilroy Semibold and Guardian Sans. The text font is Adobe Minion Pro; the heading font is Adobe Myriad Condensed; and the code font is Dalton Maag's Ubuntu Mono.

O'REILLY®

There's much more where this came from.

Experience books, videos, live online training courses, and more from O'Reilly and our 200+ partners—all in one place.

Learn more at oreilly.com/online-learning

Lightning Source UK Ltd.
Milton Keynes UK
UKHW032141040121
376416UK00009B/41